Selected Works
of
Samuel Pearce

Samuel Pearce (1766–1799)

SELECTED WORKS OF SAMUEL PEARCE

Selected Works of Samuel Pearce

Copyright © 2022 H&E Publishing
www.hesedandemet.com

Published by: H&E Publishing, West Lorne, Ontario, Canada

Reprint manager: Christopher Osterbrock

Front cover painting and frontispiece of Samuel Pearce used by kind permission of the Angus Library and Archive, Regent's Park College.

Back cover painting: Birmingham from the Dome of St Philip's Church in 1821 by Samuel Lines (1821)

Paperback ISBN: 978-1-7752633-7-1
Ebook ISBN: 978-1-77484-071-9

"This little volume comprises a delightful selection of eighteenth-century documents from Samuel Pearce. The material is warmly pastoral, profoundly biblical, insightfully doctrinal and tellingly contemporary. The publishers are to be commended for making fresh light from an old source available for readers in our day. I commend *Selected Works of Samuel Pearce* to all who love Christ and his gospel."

Edwin Ewart
Principal, Irish Baptist College

"The eighteenth-century Baptist Pastor Samuel Pearce was an exemplar of missional spirituality in the baptistic tradition, yet he is little known today. This splendid volume has the potential to introduce his writings and example to a new generation. Highly commended."

Peter Morden
Senior Pastor, Cornerstone Baptist Church, Leeds;
Distinguished Visiting Scholar, Spurgeon's College, London

"Though he lived a relatively short life, that did not stop Samuel Pearce from having a useful ministry and leaving an indelible mark upon the Particular Baptist community. Besides being a pastor and early supporter of the BMS, Pearce was eulogized as the 'seraphic Pearce'—a Baptist Brainerd. His works, largely practical, are therefore useful both for historical theology and contemporary edification."

Christopher W. Crocker
Professor of Church History, Toronto Baptist Seminary

"Vigorous conviction mingles with evident affection in this excellent collection of pieces from the soul of Samuel Pearce. Here you will find deep theology, fervent piety, profound joy and hope, social and political comment, penetrating practicality, heartfelt polemics, and evangelistic fervour, all bound together by love for God and mankind. For those who have heard of 'the seraphic Pearce,' and those who wish to be acquainted with him, here is a distant but clear glimpse of the fiery ardour that lit the heart and tongue of a man so highly esteemed in his own day, and worthy of being better appreciated in ours."

Jeremy Walker
Pastor, Maidenbower Baptist Church, Crawley;
Author, *On the Side of God: The Life and Labours of Andrew Fuller*

Contents

Foreword vii
   Michael A.G. Haykin

1. The Corporation and Test Acts 1
2. The Character and State of Departed Christians 25
3. Christian Friendship 49
4. Pearce's Description of Carey's Farewell 53
5. On Doing Good 57
6. The Scripture Doctrine of Christian Baptism 69
7. Confession of Faith 105
8. Salvation by Free Grace Alone 113
9. Ordination Sermon for W. Belsher 129
10. An Early Acquaintance with the Holy Scriptures 153
11. Motives of Gratitude 175
12. Letter to the Lascars 195

Scripture Index 203
Further reading 209

Foreword

Michael A.G. Haykin

Samuel Pearce (1766-1799) has been remembered primarily for his remarkable piety, made known especially through the memoir penned by his close friend Andrew Fuller in 1800, soon after his death. But he also left a small body of writings that were published in the 1790s: a few occasional sermons, a confession of faith, two circular letters written for the Midland Baptist Association, and an evangelistic tract. For the first time these works are gathered here between the covers of one book.

The sermons cover a range of topics throughout the years of his active ministry in the 1790s: a sermon calling for the repeal of the Corporation and Test Acts (1790), a rare political sermon by Pearce; a funeral sermon for his mentor and friend Caleb Evans (1791); a sermon defending believer's baptism by immersion (1794); an ordination sermon for William Belsher of Worcester (1796); a sermon given at a Sunday School rally (1797); and a thanksgiving sermon for British victories in the Napoleonic Wars (1798). Pearce's confession of faith is typical of such ordination statements from the long eighteenth century: the personal theological credo is in broad harmony with the theology of the *Second London Confession of Faith* (1677/1688) but expressed in the ordinand's own words. It is noteworthy that few Calvinistic Baptist authors of the eighteenth century ever cite this late seventeenth-century confession. Pearce's 1795 circular letter on salvation being by God's free grace alone is one of the few eighteenth-century documents that does so. Then, there is the evangelistic piece that was aimed at Muslim dock-workers in London and that was also distributed in India. It depicts Pearce at his best as he succinctly outlines the love of God for sinners. Finally, there are two letters that were published after his death: one to his wife Sarah describing the departure of William Carey for India and one on a topic dear to his heart, friendship.

I am deeply thankful to God for the willingness of the team at H&E publishing to make these gems from the eighteenth century available for a new generation. May the Triune God use them for his glory and our good!

Dundas, ON
Canada Day, 2022.

1
The Corporation and Test Acts[1]

1790

*"Princes have persecuted me without a cause,
but my heart stands in awe of your Word."*
Psalm 119:61

Persecution for conscience sake is nothing new. It has existed ever since virtue and vice have distinguished the characters of men. Righteous Abel was slain by his inhuman brother because "his works were righteous, and his brother's evil."[2]

We may trace the operation of the same principle throughout the history of the Jewish church. Many of the prophets of that dispensation fell victims to the infernal rage of ungodly men; and on many occasions the number of the godly was so reduced, and the revengeful spirit of the impious rose so high, that had not the former been the peculiar care of heaven, they must have been totally extirpated[3] from the earth.

David, the author of this Psalm, was no less noted for his piety than for the extraordinary revolutions which took place in his affairs; he is expressly said to be "a man after God's own heart."[4] Though the consummation of the happiness of the righteous is reserved for a future period, yet, on some occasion the Deity has been pleased to confer in this world. Therefore,

---

[1] *The Oppressive, Unjust, and Prophane Nature and Tendency of the Corporation and Test Acts Exposed, in a sermon preached before the congregation of Protestant Dissenters, February 21, 1790* (Birmingham: J. Thompson/London: J. Johnston, 1790).

[2] 1 John 3:13.

[3] *Extirpated* meaning to root out or destroy completely.

[4] 1 Samuel 13:14.

David was rewarded; for we are informed that "the Lord was with him."[5]

But from the fourteenth verse of the same chapter we learn that this very circumstance gave birth to an unconquerable hatred in Saul towards David on whose ruin he seems thenceforward determinedly bent and his courtiers (men who too often are only tools for princes) uniting with him, probably gave occasion for David's complaint in our text: "Princes have persecuted me without a cause."

That religion was the cause of his suffering persecution, is confirmed by the character of his persecutors as well as by the various expressions this chapter contains of his resolutions to persevere in the paths of godliness, notwithstanding all opposition. Therefore, with a firmness of mind which does honour to his character, he declares in the words before us that, "his heart stood in awe of God's Word."

From this view of the verse it follows: firstly, that David was persecuted on account of religion; but, secondly, David declares this was no just cause for persecution—"without cause."

The inference is easy. No difference in religious opinions and practices is a justifiable cause for persecution. But it might be enquired, "What has this to do with the subject in hand?" It is allowed that a spirit of persecution did reign in David's day, and the same existed in the days of Christ and his apostles (both Jews and Gentiles uniting in their attempts to extirpate Christianity). Yes, it is granted farther that where the intolerant spirit of Popery has prevailed there persecution prevailed also, but is it any longer known in our land? Is there such a thing as persecution realized in a kingdom so distinguished for its civil and religious liberties as England? Yes, my brethren, every conscientious Dissenter throughout the realm is to this moment a subject of per-

---

[5] 1 Samuel 18:12.

Corporation and Test Acts

secution! The laws of which I shall now attempt to expose are founded upon a principle as truly persecutive as that by which Daniel was cast into the lion's den,[6] the three children into the fiery furnace,[7] and the apostle John banished to the isle of Patmos![8] Yes, upon the same principle on which the inhuman Lewis butchered many Protestants in France! The same through which England glistened with the flames, and echoed with the groans of dying martyrs, in the days of that bloody princess (a lasting disgrace to the British throne) queen Mary.

What is persecution but imposing any hardship whatever on a man on account of his religious opinions? Have not Dissenters hardships, grievous hardships imposed upon them? Are they not the subjects of disabilities to which none but traitors should be obnoxious, merely for their religious opinions?

What then shall we say of those laws which oppress us? Can anyone deny they are founded on a persecuting principle? And does not the conduct of their supporters discover them too much influenced by an intolerant spirit?

From where arise these numerous associations to continue our grievances? To what shall we attribute the various shameful squibs from the press, and weekly declamations from the pulpit,[9] in order to inflame the minds of the ignorant, and confirm the prejudices of others, more informed but not more liberal? What

---

[6] Daniel 6:16.
[7] Daniel 3:21.
[8] Revelation 1:9.
[9] A few days before this discourse was delivered, a clergyman of this town publicly undertook to injure our cause by defaming our character, and in the warmth of his zeal against Dissenters, declared that their loyalty to the king, "had been exactly delineated with the blood of the king."

What was this but a base insinuation, that the present Dissenters are hostile to their present sovereign, and only wait an opportunity to bring king George himself on the scaffold? When this reverend gentleman, or any of his brethren in orders, can prove by facts their superior loyalty to the house of Hanover, and attachment to the present constitution, let them come forth and demonstrate it. Till then, let them not forget their duty both to preach and practice that divine command, "You shall not bear false witness against your neighbour" (Exodus 20:16).

gives birth to the language of some, that they would rather we should lose our lives than gain our ends?

Is not this the genuine effect of a Spirit congenial to Bonnors or Gardiners of old?[10] And who shall refuse such an equal share in the esteem of future generations?

It is but just, brethren, that you should be no longer misled respecting the nature and justice of our present claims.

The Test and Corporation Acts of which we complain, we oppose on the following grounds:

1. They are oppressive to us as Dissenters.
2. They are injurious and disgraceful to the nation at large.
3. They are dishonorable to God and our holy religion.

Oppressive to Dissenters

In order to your conviction of the justice of the first proposition, I need only repeat to you what they are, and lead your reflections on their extent and partiality.

What they are

The Corporation Act was passed in 1661 and provided:

> that no person or persons shall ever hereafter be placed elected, or chosen in, or to, any office or place in any corporation whatever, that shall not have, within one year next before such election or choice, have taken the sacrament of the Lord's supper, according to the rites of the church of England.[11]

But in the reign of George I, so many inconveniences were found to arise from this act, in the manner it then stood, that

---

[10] Referring to Roman Catholic Bishop of London Edmund Bonner (*c.*1500–1569) and English Bishop Stephen Gardiner (1483–1555).

[11] 13 Charles II. c. 1, § 12.

another act was passed declaring that no one should from that time be chosen to any corporate office, should incur any incapacity, disability, forfeiture, etc. unless such person be so removed, or such prosecution be commenced within six months after such persons being elected into such an office.[12]

Therefore, Dissenters are now circumstanced by this act, that should any be chosen by the suffrages[13] of the electors to fill any corporate office, and if from a consciousness of their duty and zeal for their public good, they should accept the same without conforming to the rites of the church of England, they lie open to a prosecution; even by those very same persons, or any of them, who elected them to the office.

Indeed, before the toleration act took place, they were subject to heavy penalties and disabilities, should they refuse to accept an office to which they were nominated.

Then easy was it to ruin any Dissenter, however void of offence his conduct had been, both to his God and to his country—it was only to elect him to an office—if he accepted it without qualifying (which few conscientious Dissenters would do) he must be punished for accepting it, and if he refused he must be punished for refusing it. But thank God, the lenient hand of toleration has in part wiped away this reproach from our land.

The Test Act passed in 1673 requires:

> every person who shall be admitted into any office, civil or military, or shall receive any pay, salary, fee, or wages, by reason of any patent, or grant of his majesty, or shall have command or place of trust from or under majesty, his heirs or successors, or by his or by their authority, or by authority derived from him or them, or shall be admitted into any

---

[12] 9 George I. c. 6. § 3.
[13] *Suffrages* meaning vote.

service or employment in the household of his majesty, shall take the oaths as directed in the act, and shall also receive the sacrament of the Lord's supper according to the usage of the church of England, within three months after his or their admittance into, or receiving their said authority and employment, in some public church, on some Lord's day immediately after divine service and sermon.[14]

The only alteration made in this act since its introduction, is prolonging the time allowed for qualifying from three to six months, which was done in the reign of George II. So that in all other respects it is as oppressive now as ever.

Their extent and partiality
You cannot but have remarked how oppressive these acts (particularly the latter) are on account of their extent. They exclude every nonconformist from a share in the executive part of the laws of the land and render him incapable of any office, of trust, or profit under government.

Hence, though Dissenters are obliged to contribute an equal part with their fellow-citizens towards the revenues of the Kingdom, they are wholly excluded (however deserving, or otherwise capacitated) from enjoying any office, not only of profit from, but trust with their own contributions.

And farther, as the letter of the law must be abode by, and as that expressly excludes all who are in any respect entrusted by royal authority; it exposes to the penalties of the act, many, yea, multitudes in a commercial line; for as many laws have lately been enacted, by which the vendors are obliged to take out a license for selling, and collect a duty upon certain articles such as perfumery, hats, gloves, etc. All persons of this description are now open to the prosecution of any ill-disposed person, who to

---

[14] 25 Charles II. c. 2, § 2.

injure his neighbour, or advantage himself, chooses to become informer.

Indeed, the dissenting clergy are not exempted. We are obliged to collect the tax on registers both of births and burials; in case of omission, we are fined twenty pounds for every offence, and in case of compliance, even we must take the sacrament in the church of England, according to her rites; or be open to all the penalties incurred through a breach of the Test Act.

But you enquire, what those penalties are? I reply, heavy ones indeed. Thus runs the act:

> If any person shall execute any of the said offices, or employments, without having qualified as required by the Act, and being thereon convicted, etc. he shall:
>
> 1. Be disabled from thenceforth to sue, or use any action, bill, plaint, or information, in course of law, or to prosecute any suit, in any court of equity.
>
> 2. He shall be disabled from being guardian to any child (even his own) or executor, or administrator of any person, or capable of receiving any legacy, or deed of gift.
>
> 3. He shall be incapable of bearing any office within England, Wales, or Berwick upon Tweed.
>
> 4. And shall forfeit five hundred pounds, to be recovered by him or them that shall sue for the same.

Britons! This is the glorious civil and religious liberty of which we boast—a worthy conscientious man must be ruined for doing his duty! Truly, methinks, no unprejudiced man that feels as a man would refuse to strain every nerve in order to break such shackles from his fellow citizens!

The oppression of these acts is increased by their partiality; for though extensive and unlimited with respect to the persons of the Dissenters; not so with respect to offices. Thus adds this oppressive act:

This exclusion shall not extend to the office of any high constable, petty constable, tithing man, head borough, overseer of the poor, churchwarden, surveyor of the highways, or any like inferior civil office.

So, to all "inferior civil offices" we are eligible; these we shall share with our conforming fellow subjects but from every office in the least degree desirable, we are wholly excluded.

Let Dissenters no longer, while these oppressive acts remain, boast they are the sons of Britain. No, brethren, we are rather slaves to Britain; heavy are our burdens and cruel are our task masters! Not unlike is our situation to the oppressed Israelites in Egypt, only with this difference: there was one of them admitted to be in Pharaoh's court, but not one conscientious Dissenter shall be admitted to serve the meanest office in the family of our king. Do we complain without cause? Do we groan without being burdened? It must be confessed we are heavily oppressed, our enemies themselves being judges.

Injurious and disgraceful to the nation

Notwithstanding whatever has been falsely said of our disaffection to the state, we seek a repeal of these laws not only as particularly oppressive to us as Dissenters, but as injurious and disgraceful to the nation at large.

Yes, the honour of our native land is dear to us. We Dissenters possess as noble an ardour, and as generous a zeal, for the safety, the welfare, the honour of the British nation, as ever warmed the breast of the most zealous conformist. We consider these laws as highly injurious and no less disgraceful to the land, and our concern for its prosperity urges us to seek them repealed and forgotten forever.

It cannot be supposed that one in a hundred among the present Dissenters will, or can gain any positive advantage, by the

Corporation and Test Acts

repeal of these laws—ninety-nine of a hundred must therefore be disinterested; and to what motive shall we attribute their late spirited exertions, but to a concern for the public good? Not excited by factious principles, or seditious spirits (as has been said) they are urged by better motives; they disdain such base institutions and despise their authors too.

We assert these laws are injurious to the nation at large; we prove it by declaring that they keep out from serving their country a set of men, many of whom can justly confess no superiors in capacity to fill these offices.

As a body of Dissenters we do not blush to say (because no man can disprove the assertion) that many among us are as capable of serving our country as any other of its citizens. We establish this capability by referring to the conduct, the spirited and successful conduct of many Dissenters, on many former occasions; particularly in "two rebellions the Dissenters without the exception of a single individual, showed a steady attachment to the present government." This merit none can deny to our fathers, and who can deny it is still possessed by the children?

Were not the Dissenters zealous in support of the present reigning family when the high church party were using their most nervous efforts to restore the pretender? Have they been uniform in their loyalty (notwithstanding their oppression) from the first establishment of the house of Hanover on the British throne, to the present moment? We call on our opposers to produce an instance of disaffection if they are able! On the contrary, have not many risked their lives and properties in support of the present constitution? When our adversaries can put a negative here, then let them refuse our claims.

But if these are allowed, is it not impolitic that such men should have their hands tied and feet bound when their patriotic zeal impels them to seek the public good? Does not the security of the state depend on the number of its wise, faithful, and active subjects? And is not the state injured when the number of subjects of this description is diminished?

But these acts do in fact, by restraining their exertions, diminish their number in our land; and therefore they operate injuriously to the state. Let but these acts be repealed—to its enemies it will be more formidable, and its own bosom will be enjoyed more peace.

These laws do not only injure but disgrace the nation at large. They lay it open to a charge of ingratitude in refusing those subjects whose exertions merit most, the favours which others in common enjoy. Facts have been referred to which prove that Dissenters have been not only peaceable, but active in the interests of the kingdom according to its present constitution and it is highly disgraceful to the state to treat with marked contempt its greatest friends.

These laws lay the nation open also to a charge of chicanery,[15] and deceit; because when the Dissenters, actuated by the most generous love of their country, concurred in passing the act which so oppresses them; assurances were given them that provision should afterwards be made for their relief; which indeed was done twice by the Commons and once by the Peers; and had it not been for what one calls "piece of political legerdemain"[16] would have passed into a law.

Dr. Philip Furneaux (1726–1783), in his letters to Judge Blackstone thus relates the circumstance:

> It should be observed, that the original design of the Test was, not to exclude the Protestant Dissenters, but the Papists. It was brought in by the patriots in the reign of Charles II, under their apprehensions of Popery and a Popish successor; and is styled, an "Act for preventing

---

[15] *Chicanery* meaning trickery.
[16] *Legerdemain* meaning deception.

Corporation and Test Acts

Dangers which may happen from Popish Recusants;" and the same is said to be its design in the preamble. And when, during the debate in the House of Commons, it was observed that it was drawn in such a manner as to comprehend the Protestant Dissenters, the court party endeavoured to avail themselves of that circumstance in order to defeat the bill.

But the dissenting members disappointed them by declaring that they had rather confide in the justice and generosity of parliament to pass some future bill in their favour, than be the occasion of retarding or defeating the security which the present bill was calculated to afford to the liberties of their country. And this genuine patriotism facilitated the passing of a bill, then depending in the Commons, for their relief from the penal laws; which being sent up to the Lords, and coming down with some amendments, the parliament was suddenly prorogued[17] through the resentment of the court and the intended favour to the Dissenters prevented.

And when afterwards, in 1680, a bill in favour of the Dissenters passed both houses, and lay ready for the royal assent, the court ventured upon a very extraordinary expedient; the clerk of the crown was ordered to convey away the bill; and accordingly, it was never afterwards to be found.[18]

Hence, it is evident, that the dissenting members then in the house, were not unwilling to subject themselves to a temporary evil for the sake of the public good; but, while they thus evidenced this zeal for their native land, it is no less evident they considered it as bound to release them from those evils at a proper period. That period is long since arrived; but still we have

---

[17] *Prorouged* meaning a session of Parliament discontinued without being dissolved.

[18] Philip Furneaux, *Letters to the Honorable Mr. Justice Blackstone* (Dublin, 1771), 180–181.

to groan beneath the burdens brought upon us by our truly worthy, but perhaps too incautious, ancestors. Still we have a claim on the honour of the legislature for relief; nor will the present reproach be wiped away until that relief is granted.

The Test and Corporation Acts, further, entail disgrace on the nation, as they expose it to the charge of folly and inconsistency.

And what can be a more glaring absurdity than that those very men who are considered as legally qualified for making laws, should be incapacitated for the execution of those laws when made. I mean the absurdity attending the eligibility of Dissenters to sit in parliament, while they are totally disqualified from serving even the office of a tide-waiter or exciseman; offices whose existence and regulation depend entirely on their decisions.

So surprising is this, that Bishop Sherlock, though a steady friend to these oppressive acts, declares, that "it must, upon the least reflection, appear very strange to advance a man to a share in making laws for the nation, and yet deny him all other power."[19]

Far more consistent would it be either to grant both legislative and executive power, or neither. But if long experience has proved the propriety of Dissenters being legislators, and the integrity of their conduct has been so amply demonstrated, why refuse them capacity to execute those laws their wisdom has enacted?

Again, these laws dishonour the nation, as they make an encroachment on the royal prerogative.[20]

---

[19] Thomas Sherlock, *Bishop Sherlock's Arguments Against a Repeal of the Corporation and Test Acts: Wherein Most of the Pleas Advanced in a Paper Now Circulated, Styled The Case of Protestant Dissenters, &c. are Discussed* (Oxford, 1790), 45.

[20] The king is likewise the fountain of honour, of office, and of privileges, and this in a different sense from that wherein he is stilled the fountain of justice; for here he is really the parent of them. It is impossible that government can be maintained without a due subordination of rank; that the people may know and distinguish such

The prelate before referred to, was so convinced of this, as to say, "The incapacity for offices which some lie under, in virtue of the Test Act, is in truth a restraint upon the crown."[21] Should therefore the sovereign of Britain find ever so strong a desire, to possess a conscientious Dissenter with an office, he thought him most calculated to fill—the wishes of majesty are in vain!—the man's a Dissenter! What then? He must either recant, turn hypocrite, lose his place, or ruin himself and family.

Our opponents may boast as they please, of superior loyalty and attachment to the king; but they cannot prove their assertions, without either demonstrating that limiting royal prerogative is a proof of their attachment; or else coming forward in opposition to those acts, which make this encroachment on the rights of majesty.

Important are the grounds you have already heard, [yet] we go on to justify our claims.

---

as are set over them, in order to yield them their due respect and obedience; and also that the officers themselves, being encouraged by emulation and the hopes of superiority, may the better discharge their functions; and the law supposes, that on one can be so good a judge of their several merits and services as the king himself who employs them. It has therefore entrusted him with the sole power of the conferring dignities and honours, in confidence that he will bestow them upon none but such as deserve them. From the same principle also arises the prerogative of erecting and disposing of offices; for honours and offices are in their natures convertible and synonymous.

Upon the same, or like reason, the king has also the prerogative of conferring privileges upon private persons. Such as granting place or precedence to any of his subjects as shall seem good to his royal wisdom. The king having the sole administration of the government in his hands is the best and only judge in what capacities, with what privileges, and under what distinctions his people are the best qualified to serve and act under him. A principle which was carried so far by the imperial law, that it was determined to be the crime of sacrilege, even to doubt whether the prince had appointed proper officers in the state. See William Blackstone, *Commentaries on the Laws of England: Volume 1* (Oxford, 1768), 272-273.

[21] Sherlock, *Arguments Against*, 38.

Dishonorable to God and our religion

The former we urge as men; now we come forward as Christians, and say that we pursue a repeal of the Corporation and Test Acts because they are dishonouring to God and our holy religion by prostituting the sacred ordinance of the Lord's Supper to the purpose of a qualification for civil offices.

Bishop Hoadly justly says:

> I cannot consider that as the qualification for an office, without which, the law declares all other qualifications shall signify nothing, and by virtue of which, any person who externally fulfils this law shall certainly and legally possess his post.[22]

Now it is well known that let a man be ever so wise or honest; be ever so well qualified for an office, all his other qualifications shall avail nothing, unless he takes the Sacrament according to the rites of the church of England.

It therefore follows that this holy ordinance is so debated by these acts as to become "a mere engine of state."[23] Let us only oppose the necessary purport of these acts to the original design of the institution of this Sacrament: Jesus Christ says, just before he was about to realize his last sufferings, "Do this in remembrance of me" (Luke 22:19). The Test Act in effect says, "Be-

---

[22] Benjamin Hoadly, *Refutation of Bishop Sherlock's Arguments Against a Repeal of the Test and Corporation Acts: Wherein the Justice and Reasonableness of Such a Repeal Are Clearly Evinced* (London, 1787), 8.

[23] In Christ's Church the Lord's Supper is appointed and used only for spiritual and religious ends; but, in the Church of England it is notoriously both instituted and used for political and worldly ends to qualify for a post. In the former, it is appointed with intention, and as a means of uniting all Christians, and of destroying all variance and distinctions between them. In the latter, it is appointed with intention, and as a means of discriminating and dividing Christians, and of making a distinction between one and another. See Micaiah Towgood, *A Dissent from the Church of England, Fully Justified; Being the Dissenting Gentleman's Three Letters in Answer to the Letters of the REV. John White on That Subject*, 4th ed. (Dublin, 1798), 1:18.

Corporation and Test Acts

fore you enter on any office of emolument,[24] or trust, 'Do this to qualify you for enjoying it.'"

The Scripture declares, "He that eats and drinks unworthily, eats and drinks damnation to himself,"[25] while the Test Act holds out a temptation to hundreds, thus unworthily to come and receive it. The receiver of this holy ordinance should be the possessor of pure and undefiled religion, of sacred and holy dispositions; and these should be in exercise while he surrounds the table of his dying Saviour.

But how can it be supposed that a man, when doing an act solely for civil qualification, should have his thoughts wholly occupied with divine contemplations, and be capable of discerning the Lord's body? It is most natural for our thoughts to be connected with those things which bear immediate relation to the acts we are engaged in; and when a Christian comes to the Lord's supper, from proper motives, to have his meditations assisted on the sufferings of Christ and the love of God in sending his Son into the world to save sinners;[26] that ordinance is admirably calculated to accomplish such ends. But the case is altered when he comes to qualify.

His mediations, being led to that which bears immediate relation to the act he is engaged in, we might naturally suppose are such as these: "I am about to enter on possession of some honourable or lucrative post under government. I comply with the Test Act in this instance, as a qualification, and when I have partaken of this bread and wine, I shall be installed, and confirmed in my office; such profit shall I obtain, such honours will be conferred upon me; as soon as this ceremony is over, I shall enjoy full possession of them." Therefore, he loses sight of the end of Christ's institution while he impiously profanes it.

---

[24] *Emolument* meaning a salary, fee, or profit from a position.
[25] 1 Corinthians 11:29.
[26] 1 Timothy 1:15.

Now, whatever perverts and debases any of Christ's institutions is dishonouring to God; but, such a prostitution as this does pervert and debase this sacred institution, and therefore, the application of this sacrament to civil purposes dishonours God and our holy religion. And awful it is to think! Dishonouring God is made the duty of too many Englishmen in office—made so by the laws of their country!

Every pious mind must feel a holy indignation at such perversions, and whatever their sentiments be in other matters, come forth unitedly in the common cause; and make every lawful effort for the removal of laws so dishonourable to God and detrimental to religion.

We might suppose, indeed, that the Clergy of the established Church under these impressions would lend their utmost assistance to restore that primitive simplicity to the religion of Christ, which was its first and ever will be its chief ornament; especially as they are obliged to administer this ordinance to those who apply for qualification; however convinced their consciences should be of the unfitness and unworthiness of the communicants.

It has been said, indeed, that this is optional; but whoever consults the rubric before the communion service will find that much must be proved before even the canon law will justify a refusal; and indeed, those rules are so vague and inconclusive that it is hard to say what they comprehend and what they do not. Besides, it has lately been asserted from the press (by respectable authority) that:

> the temporal courts have more than once intimated an opinion, that an action would lie against a minister, who should deny the sacrament to any person, however profligate, or in other respects objectionable, that requested it. The clergyman, therefore is the pitiable condition. A pious

man, feeling exquisitely for the interests of religion is obliged under the peril of a suit at law which may bring ruin upon himself and family, to administer the Sacrament without reserve to the most profligate unbelievers, and to wretches whose lives are a scandal to human nature; at the same time, that he is solemnly bound by the ties of duty and office to exclude them from the altar; and runs a risk of prosecution in the spiritual courts for admitting them.[27]

But, if they are silent, is that a reason we should be so too? Because they will not seek to remove this unhallowed perversion, shall we be remiss and inactive? No, rather let our activity put their supineness[28] to the blush; let us make every just exertion in behalf of the cause of Englishmen! The cause of Christianity! The cause of God!

Objections
Having set before you the principle motives which induce us to seek a repeal of these oppressive acts, it may be necessary to state, and briefly reply to some objections which have been made to repeal:

1. Many say, "These laws are never put in force, and therefore why this clamour to redress an ideal evil?"

I reply, the objection is indefensible, for there is an action now pending in law, brought against the Mayor of Nottingham for his acceptance of that office without taking the Sacrament to qualify.

---

[27] "In the Christian Church, no openly debauched, or scandalously wicked person, has a right to come to the table of the Lord, or to partake of its provisions; but in the Church of England, if such a person has a commission from the king, in the army, or the fleet, or any other profitable post, this gives him a right to come to the communion table, a right to demand the holy elements at the priest's hands, as a qualification for his post." Towgood, *Dissent from the Church of England*, 1:18.

[28] *Supineness* meaning inactivity or slothfulness.

But supposing they never have been executed, can it be imputed to any other cause than this—that men of the most depraved minds and manners are not so far degenerated as to disgrace themselves by appearing in so shameful a cause. And surely, when laws become useless by the general content of the nation, there can be no show of reason for retaining them.

2. It is objected that the church is so intimately connected with the state that the safety of the latter depends upon the preservation of the former, and that to provide for this, none should be advanced to offices of trust, or emolument, but such as are of the established religion.

But the fallacy of this is demonstrated, first, by an appeal to the conduct of other nations to persons of different religious persuasions, many of which have advanced Dissenters from the established religion to the highest posts of honour, and emolument in the state. And the good effects which have attended such liberal conduct makes it apparent that the constitution of England can be in no danger from the disannulling of these distinctions.

Second, by an appeal to the conduct of Dissenters in support of the present constitution on past occasions. None can deny that have proved themselves steady friends to it, when conformists, nursed in its bosom, and enjoying favours conferred with a lavish hand upon them, have proved vipers, striving to destroy the hand that cherished them.

And as to the church itself, I might say, it probably owes its very existence to Dissenters; for had they not repeatedly stood in the gap, the established church in England, in its present form, would have to all human appearance perished forever, unless in the pages of history. And how are we repaid? With the base coin of penalties, forfeitures, disabilities, exclusions, and contempt.

3. Another objection has been raised, namely, that the preservation of religion depends on the state's distinguishing

Corporation and Test Acts

those who are of its own religion in order to discourage error and promote piety.

But, pray, can there be no religion out of the Church of England? Has this church separated from the Pope, only to assume a papal infallibility to herself? Is she the only true standard of doctrine and discipline? By whose inspiration were articles, homilies, book of common prayer, etc. drawn up? Can she assert they were formed under the unerring influence of divinity? No doubt their compilers believed all consistent with the will of God; but was not this judgement formed in opposition to the established church to which themselves had been subject? Did they not claim a right to judge for themselves in the dissent from the Catholic church? And will they deny us the same privileges?

Thank God! We have the Scriptures in our own hands, and its decisions alone we will abide by. In the words of our text we declare, "Our hearts stand in awe of God's Word."

If this objection be admitted, then it must be allowed that were Mahometanism[29] the established religion, or Judaism the established religion of the land; we ought to be persecuted, unless we would turn Mahometans or Jews. The same principle would justify every government, whether Pagan, Papal, Mahometans, or Jewish, in persecuting the members of the established church of England should they the superiority in numbers as the members of that church have to go upon to justify their conduct to Dissenters. But the kingdom of Christ is not of this world. It was not introduced, nor was it ever benefited by the secular arm.

Civil distinctions may make men hypocrites, but can never make them Christians. God, and a man's conscience are the only parties to be concerned in a man's religion; and when anyone becomes a member of any religious society for the lure of emol-

---

[29] *Mahometanism* meaning Islam.

ument; he will eventually prove a disgrace to that society who tempted him to sacrifice his conscience for their favours.

No one who is acquainted with the sudden change which took place in the state of Christianity when particular tenets first received distinguished support from majesty, can deny, that the first attempt to establish it by the civil arm proved eventually more injurious to its interests than all the rage of its adversaries, and the consequence persecution it experienced for three centuries before.

A partial protection of Christianity is an assumption of the prerogative of Deity: the truths of God have omnipotence on their side, and so aided they can never totally fall—Uzziah of old was assuming the place of God when he put forth his hand to support the ark,[30] and fell a victim to his own presumptions. May a similar fate be averted from all whose conduct is similar to his in our day.

Conclusion

You have now heard a statement of our case, the nature and reasons of our demands, and the futility of the objections raised against them. No longer misrepresent us; no longer hear our characters calumniated, nor our claims censured. Be bold for your country and your God. If the oppression of a respectable part of your fellow-citizens has no weight with you, if the honour of your native land warms not your heart in the cause, yet remember what we seek bears a close connection with the honour of the religion we all profess. And if we are Christians, let us manifest it by using our best efforts to rescue the institutes of Christianity from appropriation to civil purposes. At the least, let us one and all pray for the dawn of that glorious day when all invidious distinctions between Christians shall cease; when Ju-

---

[30] 2 Samuel 6:6.

dah shall no more vex Ephraim, nor Ephraim envy Judah. Let peace be upon Israel,[31] when pure and unadulterated religion, both in principle and practice shall extend from sea to sea, and shore to shore, until all the nations of the earth become united in one common bond of Christian charity. With respect to the object we have in view, it is our duty and privilege to hold up one another's hands in so glorious a cause. But after using every proper means, let us contentedly leave the issue with God; he is the disposer of all events, it is for us to be resigned to his will.

Should it please him to crown our present exertions with success, let us pray that the enlargement of our liberties may be attended with the advance of his glory.

But should we be disappointed, let us be still satisfied with the wisdom of his disposals; remembering that though for the present our wishes may be frustrated, from the face of the times it cannot be so long. No brethren, many who now oppose may live to regret that they have not supported our present claims, and be urged on with double pleasure to hail the reign of universal liberty over our happy isle—yes, themselves to be most forward in erecting her banner, and offering themselves her willing votaries. But whether this should be in our day or not, we may be well assured that the present era, when so noble a stand has been made for the rights of mankind, will long live distinguished in the annals of the British empire, and future generations will rise up and call us blessed, as the assertors of that liberty which they will then enjoy.

In the interval, let nothing shake our fidelity to our God. Let us never sacrifice the peace of our bosoms or our duties to our Maker at the shrine of avarice or fame. Let the temptation be ever so great, still let us hold fast our integrity; ever having it in our power to say in the language of David, "If we are persecuted

---

[31] Isaiah 11:13.

it is without a cause, our hearts still stand in awe of God's Word."[32] No, blessed Redeemer! We will never prostitute the memorials of your death and sufferings to obtain secular advantages. We will stand in awe of your Word which says, "as often as you do this, do it in remembrance of me."[33] We will never go to Calvary to seek temporal emoluments! Never will we visit Gethsemane with our feet, while our hearts are set on our idols! We will never make your tomb the path to earthly preferment! We will rather endure shame, and disgrace, contempt, and persecution, than profane with unhallowed hands and lips your sacred institutions. If through a zeal for your honour our enemies triumph over us, we will not return railing for railing, but teach them by our conduct that going to the holy altar with suitable dispositions tends to conform us more to the blessed pattern you have exhibited in your own person, for our imitation; and inclines us uniformly to obey that Christian precept, "When you are reviled, revile not again."[34]

This, brethren, be your determined resolution, that let what will be the issue, your hearts shall stand in awe of God's Word. And while we are justly contending for our external liberties; let us not forget to be continually aiming at a perfect deliverance from the bondage of iniquity; let us be watchful, that sin has not dominion over us,[35] but that we make daily advances towards that perfection of freedom from sin, ignorance, and affliction, which awaits all the godly in the world to come.

It has no connection with our eternal welfare, whether we enjoy the liberty of churchmen, or are restrained with the oppressed Dissenters here; so, we have but a name and a place in the church triumphant.

---

[32] A slight modification of Psalm 119:61.
[33] Luke 22:19.
[34] 1 Peter 2:23.
[35] Romans 6:14.

It matters not much, compared with this, whether our names are enrolled in the registers of corporations, or offices of profits or honour, under civil government; so we have but our names written in the Lamb's book of life,[36] and are prepared for and by-and-by are introduced to immortal and never fading glories in the world to come. There no more to complain of oppression, persecution, or disgrace, but exalted to the highest honours, enjoy uninterrupted tranquility and joys, which know neither bound nor end.

---

[36] Revelation 21:27.

2
The Character and State of Departed Christians[1]

1791

The death of great and good men is a matter of no small concern to the truly pious of every denomination; and it seems as useful as it is natural to notice such events from the pulpit. Not merely as a token of respect to their memories, but to calm the minds of afflicted friends to justify the dispensations of God, and to excite those who remain to emulate the character of those who are taken away.

Our dear departed brother, the Rev. Dr. Evans, was a man both good and great. His praise is in all the churches, the memory of his worth still lives in the hearts of all who knew him, and the news of his removal produced, in many other minds, sensations like those the prophet felt of old when he thus lamented his departing master: "My father! My father! The chariots of Israel, and the horsemen thereof!"[2]

Convinced that an attempt to improve this painful providence will be acceptable to you, as well as gratifying to myself—I know of no Scripture more suited to direct such an effort than that you find recorded.

"Our friend Lazarus sleeps" (John 11:2).

---

[1] *Reflections on the Character and State of Departed Christians: In A Sermon Occasioned by the Decease of the Rev. Caleb Evans* (Birmingham, 1791).

[2] 2 Kings 2:12.

You need not be made acquainted with the particulars of the event to which these words relate. You remember that in Bethany, a small town a few miles distant from Jerusalem, there dwelt a very happy, pious family consisting of a brother and two sisters. They were very intimate with our Lord, and their house was the place of his residence as often as he came that way. Jesus Christ had a strong affection for this family—he loved Martha, her sister Mary, and Lazarus.

It seems Lazarus was afflicted with a disease which terminated in his death; but before his death, his sisters went to our Lord, who was then the other side of Jordan, saying, "Lord, behold he whom you love is sick."[3] For this reason he chose neither to heal him of his disease nor visit him in his affliction, but abode two days still in the same place where he was. He knew that although his permitting the death of Lazarus would occasion much temporary distress to his surviving friends, yet it would eventually tend to the establishment of his divine mission, and therefore to the glory of God, on which account he says to his disciples, "For your sake I am glad, to the end that you may believe."[4]

At the expiration of these two days, he proposes to his disciples to visit Judea again but they, recollecting that they were in danger of losing their master through the malice of the Jews the last time they were there, objected to his proposal. Jesus Christ urges the propriety of attending to our duty, whatever opposition may be made, or danger anticipated and, probably to induce them to accompany him, he adds, "Our friend Lazarus sleeps; but I go that I may awake him out of sleep." This is explained in verse 14, for he says plainly, "Lazarus is dead."

---

[3] John 11:3.
[4] John 11:15.

Character and State of Departed Christians

There appears a remarkable evidence of Christ's omniscience in this declaration. The messengers sent by Mary and Martha only gave information of his sickness, yet we find Jesus is now acquainted with his death. This, probably among other occurrences of the same nature, was present to Peter's mind when, with devout humility, he said after our Lord's resurrection, "Lord, you know all things."[5]

The figure here used by our Lord to express the death of Lazarus was familiar among the Jews. When God foretold the death of Moses, he says, "Behold you will sleep with your fathers."[6] And David, entreating divine interpolation, says, "Lighten my eyes O Lord, lest I sleep the sleep of death."[7] Also, as it was not infrequent among Jews, for it was afterwards adopted by Christians, Paul says, "Those that sleep in Jesus will God bring with him."[8] Even among ancient Christians, perhaps from this and familiar pages, denominated their places of burial cemeteries, or sleeping places.

It cannot then be asserted that the term was only applicable to the fate in which Lazarus was, but it applies to the situation of every good man who has passed the gates of death.

We shall consider our text, therefore, in the following manner: firstly, to assist our reflections on the character of true Christian living; secondly, to consider the state of a true Christian after death.

The real character of true Christian living

Firstly, the words present us with the real character of true Christian living. "Our friend," says Jesus. Friendship is in itself a pleasing subject both for reflection and discourse, especially

---

[5] John 21:17.
[6] Deuteronomy 31:16.
[7] Psalm 13:13.
[8] 1 Thessalonians 4:14.

pious friendship, but that friendship to which our thoughts are now to be directed is friendship with Jesus Christ.

A high esteem for Christ

Friendship with Jesus Christ evidences itself in a high esteem for his person. Lazarus indeed had opportunities of discovering his esteem for Christ in a way which we have not; namely, by accommodating him while he was in the flesh. Was he persecuted in Jerusalem? He might go to Bethany—there he found Lazarus and his sisters ready to receive him, and afford a welcome shelter from the rage and malice of his foes. Did he stand in need of food or lodging? Here he found attendance which approached the point of needing restraint. Had his journeys occasioned his fatigue? Here the tears of affection flowed in torrents to wash his feet, while Mary neither thought it too mean to wipe them with the hairs of her head, nor too extravagant to anoint them with the costliest perfume. Did the rest of mankind reject his doctrines and insult his person? Here he found Mary ready to sit at his feet and listen to the gracious words which proceeded out of his mouth. No wonder Jesus loved Mary, and her sister, and Lazarus; no wonder Lazarus and his sisters loved Jesus.

But though we, my brethren, can no longer entertain this noble guest in person, yet, by entertaining the highest esteem for his character—and maintaining his personal honors—we may still prove our friendship.

When the Judean world despised Christ, and called him the carpenter's son, Lazarus and his sisters owned him as their Lord, and gave the most public proofs of their respect. Nor shall we, if we are true friends to Christ, be backward to avow his cause and maintain his honors.

A man who thinks meanly of Christ deserves not to bear his name. A mind enlightened into a knowledge of the gospel cannot but revere him who shines throughout the whole as the brightness of the Father's glory, and the express image of his person. He must be adored as God over all, trusted in as the great high priest of the Christian profession, and obeyed as King in Zion and the sole legislator of his church.

With these views of Christ, is it possible his friends should be indifferent while the majesty of his nature, the efficacy of his sacrifice, or the glory of his gospel are opposed and despised by nominal professors? It is an insult to the sacred name of friendship to suppose it for a moment. Willing to endure the cross himself, the true Christian cannot bear without poignant grief and holy zeal, to see his Saviour thus crucified afresh and put to open shame.

In the present day we have constant opportunities of seeking and supporting the dignity of the Son of God. In this age, perhaps above all others, those who call themselves his friends are most assiduous in lessening his honors and insulting his character. Infidels and Deists have been outdone, or else see their efforts are needless. In the last age, the glories of Immanuel became the sport of Atheists, or the ostensible ground on which the sons of Deism opposed Christianity—but they have now quitted the field. Professing Christians, with the cross on their banners, have unsheathed the sword against the Lord of Glory, and Christ has been wounded in the house of his avowed friends! O how does it behove us, if we are true friends to him, to abound yet more and more in all our zealous and Scriptural efforts to fight the good fight of faith, and contend earnestly for those glorious truths respecting the person of Jesus, which were, by himself and his own apostles, delivered to the saints.

Affection for his people
Friendship for Christ will discover itself in a cordial affection for his followers. Hence, says Jesus, "our friend Lazarus." This

good man did not confine his regard to Christ himself, but extended his kindness and care to his disciples too.

This has been since proposed as an indisputable evidence of real friendship with Christ: "By this we know we are passed from death to life, because we love the brethren."[9] Pompous titles, splendid stations, unbounded wealth, extensive power, or universal knowledge, are the objects of worldly admiration. These only serve to direct the carnal heart where to place its friendship and solicit its return. But a Christian, looking beyond the external glitter of wealth, and deaf to the noisy gust of vain applause, seeks the society and cultivates the friendship of the disciples of the lowly Jesus—the man, and not the station, he admires—and justly thinks to himself, "A Christian is the highest kind of man."

To select those whom Christ has selected, to lend assistance to those for whom his Redeemer bled, and to associate with those who are to be his companions forever, will be his chief delight. In the Christian he views Christ himself, and whether he meets him derided or applauded, abased or exalted, he will love the Christian for Christ's sake, and consider that whatever he does to the disciple, his master considers as done to himself.

Zealous concern for his interest

A true Christian, or friend to Christ, will be much concerned for, and do all his endeavour to promote the cause and interest of Christ. Nothing affords the Christian more joy than to hear of Christ's success; as Barnabas was glad when he saw the grace of God at Antioch,[10] and Judah rejoices when the salvation of the Lord comes out of Zion.[11] On the other hand, nothing gives him more pain than to hear of its decline; as with David, so he too

---

[9] 1 John 3:14.
[10] Acts 11:23.
[11] Psalm 53.

can appeal to God and say, "Lord, am I not grieved with those that rise up against you? I count them my enemies."[12]

The feelings and interest of a Christian's heart will provoke the activity of his hands. His time, his powers, his fortune, and, yes, life itself, will be a sacrifice small in his esteem so that the cause of Christ may be promoted. Paul said, "I count not my life dear, so I may fulfill the ministry I have received of the Lord."[13]

False are all those professions of friendship made by men that cease in the day of adversity, or are suspended in the hour of necessity. The juvenile lawyer could call Jesus, "Lord," and ask his instructions but, being told to part with his possessions for the sake of Christ's poor, went away sorrowful, and thereby proved his insincerity.[14] Too many resemble him in the present day. They will call Jesus, "Lord," but will afford no assistance to erect his kingdom, and even feel themselves unconcerned whether it prospers or declines. Let all remember that indifferency of heart in the activity of life respecting the cause of Christianity in the world, leaves no room to hope that they shall ever share its blessings. Let them not imagine they shall receive anything from the Lord, for with what measure out, it shall be measured unto them again.[15]

We have seen then, that only such as possess a high esteem for Christ, a cordial affection for his people, and manifest a zealous concern for his interest, can reasonably hope that Jesus will own them as his friends at a future day.

The life of Caleb Evans

Such a one both we, and Jesus too, recognized in our dear departed brother. Few men discovered more genuine regard to the

---

[12] Psalm 139:21.
[13] Acts 20:24.
[14] Matthew 19:22.
[15] Matthew 7:2.

person, followers, and interest of Christ, from the time he first felt the saving influence of religious truth to the period of his departure.

Caleb Evans was born in the year 1737 under the care of a pious parent, and here his mind not only became habituated to morality, but in early life gave satisfactory evidences of the most genuine piety. Desirous of doing good to souls, he diligently applied himself to theological studies and, having done himself and tutors honor by his assiduity and rapid improvement, he appeared in the character of a gospel minister. Soon after, at the pressing request of the congregation meeting in Broadmead, Bristol, became an assistant to his father, the late Rev. Hugh Evans, there, being then about the age of 22 years. After the expiration of eight years he took upon him, in conjunction with his father, the office of pastor over that church. This honorable office he filled with the most distinguished reputation till he was removed to the general assembly and church of the firstborn, whose names are written in heaven, on the 9th of August last, aged 54 years.

His character

How pleasing the review of his character! Eminently a friend to Jesus—the honors of his person, the deity of his nature, and the glory of his mediatorial office—he warmly and ably defended both in public discourses and private conversation. Controversies he never courted, yet never flighted them when he thought it needful either to speak or write in defence of the truth. Neither personal friendship, eminence of rank, nor the literary skill of his opponents repressed his zeal for the Saviour's glory—but here I need not enlarge as his works praise him in the gates. The writings he has left behind him say all this, and more, in behalf of his profound veneration for Jesus Christ.

Nor was he deficient in his regard for the sincere followers of the Lamb, but was a friend to them. He despised no man but loved all as the creatures of God, and was at all times happy to promote their welfare, but especially he loved the household of faith. In him the indigent[16] believer always found a friend ready to weep in his sorrows, direct him in his difficulties, and assist him in all his necessities. Many instances are still present to the recollection of his friends, wherein the fatherless have found in him a father, and by extraordinary exertions he has made the widow's heart to sing for joy.

For the interest of Christ at large, how great his concern it is impossible to say. Providence called him to move in a large and public sphere and for his various duties therein, he was eminently fitted; discharging them not merely as the incumbrances of his station, but as the privileges of his existence.

Besides the peculiar duties of his pastoral office, the affairs over which he presided included the principle direction of the western association of the academy[17] (which is very large), and his pious soul was happy or distressed as the cause of his master flourished or decayed.

His writings

Many circumstances of his life might, if necessary, be introduced wherein he discovered the greatest tenderness of mind for Zion's prosperity and proved how anxious he was to have gospel truth remain uncorrupted, and gospel tempers and conduct invariably manifested. For, well aware that a church or minister would never prosper while he or they maintained opinions derogatory to the honor of Jesus Christ, he not only preached frequently on the subjects of Christ's divinity and atonement, but sought more

---

[16] *Indigent* meaning poor, or needy.
[17] Caleb Evans was the President of Bristol Baptist Academy.

extensive usefulness by publishing some of his compositions on those subjects.

The last work of this kind he ever published has been greatly blessed to the establishment of many in the truths of the gospel and, if any of my hearers wish to pursue a work pregnant with piety, and which support the important doctrines of the cross on Scriptural foundations, and written in an experimental manner, I would recommend to them Dr. Evans' four sermons on the atonement entitled, *Christ Crucified*, which will amply repay the purchase and the perusal to every serious mind.

In this latter publication we discover how firm his mind had been kept in that great leading truth of the gospel, the doctrine of the atonement, concerning which he thus writes to his people:

> It is now thirty years since you first called me to become one of your ministers, in connection with my honored father. I began my ministry amongst you, as some of you may possibly remember, with a discourse from those words of Paul to the Corinthians, "I determined not to know anything among you, save Jesus Christ, and him crucified."[18] And now that I am advancing fast to the close of my life and ministry, and have reason to expect that at no very distant period, I shall be numbered with my fathers and called to give my account, I wish these sermons to stand as a humble memorial of my firmest adherence to the same doctrine which has ever been uniformly and zealously preached to you by each of your present, as well as former ministers. I desire to die testifying that this is the gospel of the grace of God, wherein you stand. God forbid you should receive any other, though an angel from heaven, were it possible, should preach it to you.[19]

---

[18] 1 Corinthians 2:2.
[19] Caleb Evans, *Christ Crucified* (Bristol: William Pine, 1789), 8.

Character and State of Departed Christians

By this address, written about two years before his death, we see that his investigation of gospel truth, so far from weakening his faith in the doctrine of the atonement, only served to establish him more firmly in its divinity and importance. Of such consequence did he consider it that in the same work he says:

> To me it appears with a blaze of the brightest evidence, to be the grand distinguishing doctrine of the New Testament, the glory of Christianity, and the highest and most illustrious display of the divine perfections and character. I verily believe that the general rejection of this doctrine would involve in it, eventually, the destruction of all serious and practical religion.[20]

I make these quotations as a reply to a late publication, wherein an anti-trinitarian writer of note has asserted that the ablest, wisest, and most pious Christians, were of his opinion respecting the person and work of Christ.[21] While Dr. Evans is allowed to be pious, wise, and good, that acknowledgment will contradict an assertion so bold and unjust. His living and dying

---

[20] Evans, *Christ Crucified*, 5.
[21] See Joseph Priestley, "Address to the Jews," in *The Evidence of the Resurrection of Jesus Considered in a Discourse ... To which is Added an Address to the Jews* (Birmingham, 1791), xvi. His words are, "The belief of the divine unity, and also that of the proper humanity of Christ, are not now the private opinions of a few persons only, which some time ago they were almost afraid to avow; but they are publicly professed by great numbers the most respectable for their ability, their learning, and their piety among Christians." It is evident to everyone acquainted with the Socinian controversy, that the Doctor here meant to describe persons of his own religious tenets, though he evidently insinuates that we oppose the unity of the Godhead, and the proper humanity of Christ. It is known to the world, that whilst, in obedience to the authority of revelation, we maintain there are three who bear record in heaven, the Father, Word, and Holy Spirit; yet we do unreservedly declare and believe these three are one. And although we believe that our Lord Jesus Christ, as to his divine nature, is God over all, blessed forever, yet we unequivocally affirm, that as concerning the flesh, he came from the fathers, that he was "bone of our bone, and flesh of our flesh" and that in our nature, though in a glorified state, he now reigns in heaven as the great head of the church. Though misrepresentation may serve a cause, it can surely never do it credit.

testimony opposed the sentiments of Socinus as unscriptural, unsafe, and inimical to morality itself.

Evans now rests

Such a light in the gospel hemisphere, we might have thought, would have been long continued to illuminate and refresh the churches! Such a friend to Christ, to his people, to his cause, we would have wished long to have enjoyed! But wise heaven has otherwise decreed. This star will shine on earth no more! This friend shall no more exert himself on earth for Jesus! No, our friend Evans sleeps. Death has closed his eyes in peaceful slumber to open them no more on terrestrial scenes. In the cold grave he lies, while we drop the tributary tear over our departed friend, by him unheeded.

Death is a gloomy subject. Reflection on it chills the mind and appalls human nature. To be torn from our dear connections, to quit those scenes which have afforded us so much delight, to become tenants of those dreary habitations is surely the repository of man in his most abject state. To dwell with skulls, monuments, and worms; to part with all the glory of our nature, to be separated from intelligence, yea, from animation itself; to be constrained to say to corruption, "You are our father," and to acknowledge the worm for our brother and sister! At all this, no wonder nature shudders.

But our Saviour, in condescension to our feelings, calls upon us to view it under a softer representation. To consider it not as annihilation, but as a sleep; so that as we in imagination pass by the tomb of our deceased brother, we will calm our minds by reflecting thus: "Our friend Evans is not dead, but sleeps. This is his couch, here let him rest from the fatigues of the day of life till the night of time be past, and the eternal morning dawn."

Three ideas of the state of departed Christians
Sleep gives us three ideas of the state of departed Christians:

It leads our thoughts to inactivity
Firstly, it leads our thoughts to inactivity. As during the season of repose, we forget our usual exertions, and our members are no more employed in labor, but a general indolence prevails; so, at death all the former efforts of the Christian cease.

The pious man is no longer found pouring out his soul to God in private prayer. The walls of his closet, which have heretofore witnessed his devout supplications, fervent petitions, and grateful praise, now witness them no more.

The pious master, husband, or parent, no more raises his domestic altars to the God of his life, and no longer leads the devotions of his household. His children and servants no more listen to his salutary instructions, nor weep beneath his affectionate exhortations. No more does the friend of his bosom hear him pour the balm of pious consolation in the afflictive hour.

The pious minister no more enters the pulpit, nor charms the ears, nor warms the hearts of his auditory by his zealous and affectionate delivery of gospel truth. No longer does he enter the sacred laver and there consecrates the seals of his ministry to the obedience of Christ. No longer does he meet with his beloved flock at the table of the Lord, breaking the bread of life to them, and directing their minds and their affections to the Lamb of God who takes away the sin of the world.

The pious author no more appears the champion of heavenly truth, nor longer enters the lists with the public enemies of Christ and his gospel. The truth-fraught page, the animating sentiment, the convincing argument, the harmony of just and graceful composition no longer flows from his well-directed pen.

The pious friend no more visits the social circle where before with cheerful decorum he regulated the pleasures of friendly hearts.

The pious tutor no more trains up the youthful mind in habits of scientific and religious truth. His exertions for their improvement in useful knowledge and heavenly virtue, and his efforts to fit them for usefulness in the various stations wherein providence might in future place them, cease—and cease forever.

The removal of a man in any of these stations would be felt, and felt severely, but the removal of our friend Evans makes us feel and bemoan the loss of one who filled them all. In him the children mourn an indulgent father, the servants bewail an affectionate master, and the widow weeps yes, these eyes have seen her tears—she weeps the loss of an invaluable husband.

Zion sits in the dust, bemoaning, because he is not, and almost refuses to be comforted:

> The beauty of Israel is slain; how are the mighty fallen! The elders have ceased from the gate, the young men from their music, the joy of our heart is ceased, our dance is turned into mourning, the crown is fallen from our head. For this our heart is faint; for these things our eyes are dim, because of the mountain of Zion which is desolate.[22]

Yes, he who late ascended his pulpit as his throne, and like a faithful ambassador of Christ, besought sinners to be reconciled to God, has relinquished his wonted labors, and has ceased to stand pleading the cause of heaven with rebellious man. The terrors of the law shall no more arouse the careless, nor the mild accents of the gospel dissolve the stony heart.

---

[22] 2 Samuel 1:19; Lamentations 5:14.

What thing shall I take to witness for you? What thing shall I liken to you, O daughter of Jerusalem? What shall I equal to you, that I may comfort you, O virgin daughter of Zion? For your breach is great, like the sea and who can heal you?[23]

His pen shall be no more employed in defending the sacred truths of the inspired volume. The wisdom and equity of the divine conduct, the awful depravity of human nature, the riches of sovereign grace, the dignity of Immanuel's person, the efficacy of his sacrifice, and the personality and deity of the Holy Spirit, which have been so clearly exhibited and ably maintained by him, shall no more receive elucidation and proof from his hands.[24] And how many friendly hearts will unite to lament his loss, whose presence was at once both their joy and their guide! Perhaps no man in his social intercourse ever steered more happily free of the extremes of morose reserve and foolish levity—cheerful, but not light, would that society be where our friend Evans was.

But to the pupils who, under his care, were trained or training up for the gospel ministry, how great his loss it is impossible to describe. We feel it, but though he taught us much, he never taught us to express the grief his removal would cost us. He knew well how to gain our affections, while he secured our respect—at once we loved the friend, and venerated the tutor. So mildly he corrected our mistakes, and so gladly marked our improvement, that the reverberated happiness which our attention to his wise instructions afforded him, was one great stimulus to our diligence. Nor was it possible that a worthy pupil could ever be beneath his care, who did not feel his esteem for Dr. Evans

---

[23] Lamentations 2:13.
[24] See his *Address* to the serious and candid professors of Christianity. Also, his two sermons on the Scripture doctrine of *The Deity of the Son and Holy Spirit.*

rise, as his acquaintance with his character became more intimate.

Nor did his concern for our happiness terminate with the years of our pupilage. How many of us can witness the pains it cost him to fix us in those situations for which he thought our various capacities, definitions, and improvements fitted us! How many wise and pious cautions has he given us respecting our conduct as men, as Christians, and as ministers! What journeys would he take to assist in our settlement with a people! What undisguised pleasure did he express when he discovered a prospect of our future usefulness and comfort! Surely, we cannot do less than revere his memory. May we have grace to profit by his pious counsels!

As a public character, his activity was well known. Your hearts, and the hearts of thousands more, will much longer perpetuate his worth than this unworthy tribute to his memory. A recollection of his kindness must be now present to many in this congregation, since but one year has measured its course since he took a public part in the solemn services accompanying my union to you as a pastor. I hope I shall never forget his truly affectionate address to me on that occasion, but, "by the manifestation of truth, commend myself to every man's conscience in the sight of God."[25]

You remember also, my worthy brethren, who on that day were invested with the office of deacons in this society, with what simplicity and affection he set before you both the honors and duties of your pious functions. Nor can the members of this church forget the pleasures of that day, to which he so largely contributed in conjunction with our late dear and honored

---

[25] 2 Corinthians 4:2—The passage on which Dr. Evans grounded his charge at the ordination.

brother, Mr. Hall of Amsby.[26] Ah! Little did we then think that, before another twelve months came, those two great men of God should be no more. But they are gone. Our friend Hall is removed, and our friend Evans also sleeps.

I reflect with solemnity that the hand then placed on this unworthy head, expressive of his approbation of the union which then commenced, is now mouldering in the dust. Those lips which conveyed such salutary and affectionate instruction to my heart are now sealed up forever. Yes, his activity in this world for God, for us, and for Zion at large is over.

A cessation from painful suffering
But, secondly, sleep affords us another idea, that it is not only a cessation from pleasing activity, but also from painful suffering. It gives us the idea of rest and, in this respect, is analogous to death. "I heard a voice from heaven, saying, blessed are the dead which die in the Lord, from henceforth; yea, says the Spirit, that they may rest from their labors."[27]

Our respected friend whose loss we now deplore, amiable as he was in his manners and useful as he was in his life, was not exempt from many sorrows—especially towards the close of his days. I had almost numbered the sympathy of his heart among the causes of his distress, since few men possessed so much of the delicacies of sympathetic sensibility, or shared so much in other's woe as he. He did truly weep with those who wept.

His many and great exertions greatly debilitated his nervous system so that, for some years past, his health has suffered vari-

---

[26] Rev. Mr. [Robert] Hall preached to the church on the same occasion. He expired almost suddenly, on Lord's-day evening of March 31, 1791. A funeral discourse delivered by Mr. [John] Ryland, of Northampton; to which are annexed, the oration at the grave, by Mr. [Andrew] Fuller, and an account of the rise of Amsby Church, and its successive ministers, particularly of its late venerable pastor, has been since published; to which the reader is referred for a fuller account of this most excellent man.
[27] Revelation 14:13.

ous interruptions, to which trials of a more afflictive nature have also largely contributed.

About twenty-one months ago, he returned from supplying this congregation. He arrived home late in the evening and found all well, but the first intelligence he received on the following day was that his eldest son, just then established in business, had been seized with a violent fit in the night and was found breathless in his room in the morning. He tenderly loved his children, and so severe a stroke made a deep wound in such a heart as his.

To this must be added a sudden and painful event arising from his religious connections which taught him, by distressing experience, that not the strongest friendship, purity of intention, nor guarded conduct, can at all times be free from unkindness and censure; but friendship is impatient of unkindness, and conscious integrity starts at unmerited reproach. Surprise and grief overcame a constitution already injured by unusual exertion and sudden affliction, and no doubt accelerated his dissolution.

His habit became more relaxed till about three months since, when an unexpected paralytic stroke for a few days deprived him of the powers of speech and motion. By degrees, he recovered at that time so as to be able to converse freely and take occasional exercise. His friends marked with gratitude his returning health, and flattered themselves he would soon be restored to their highest wishes. Then on Lord's-day, the 7th of August, he proposed preaching in the evening to a favourite congregation at Downend, near Bristol, and said he hoped he should be able to speak to them for half an hour—but, Lord, how precarious is our state, and uncertain our designs! About two o'clock the same day he had a second seizure, easy in its approach, but mortal in its effects. Then, being put in his bed, he neither spoke a word nor altered his position till the following Tuesday when he died, or rather, finally fell asleep.

Character and State of Departed Christians

For some time before he had expressed his wish for departure, and seemed to possess a premonition of its approach. On the last day of his administering the ordinance of the Lord's supper, he told the communicants at the table that he longed to depart and be with Christ, repeating with energy, "It is far better."[28] Indeed, the extract you have heard from his late publication indicates his expectations that he should not long survive that work, and many occasional expressions which he dropped confirmed his own opinion of his approaching dissolution.[29]

Perhaps a peculiar depression of spirits and lassitude of body occasioned his suspicions; but with him, the headache, and the heartache too, are over. "Our friend Evans sleeps,"—no bereaving providence, no unkind reflections, no bodily afflictions, can disturb him now.

> Softly his fainting head he lay
> Upon his Maker's breast;
> His Maker kissed his soul away,
> And laid his flesh to rest.[30]

The resurrection of the dead

Thirdly, let us not forget that although the members of his body are now inactive, though the places that knew him once know him now no more, a season draws near when he shall awake and rise from his dusty bed—the mouldering tomb wherein he lies. Death is represented by sleep particularly in reference to the resurrection of the dead. Yes, while we, like Martha, go to Jesus and say, "Lord, if you had been here—if you had exerted your

---

[28] Philippians 1:23.

[29] To one affecting expression of this nature I was an ear witness. About a fortnight before his death, the caretaker enquired whether he had registered some burials, to which he replied, "Yes, and I will return the book to you tomorrow, for you will soon have my name to register."

[30] Isaac Watts (1674–1748), "Lord, 'Tis an Infinite Delight."

power, our brother had not died."³¹ We hear him replying to us, as he did to her, "Your brother shall rise again." "I," says he, "am the resurrection and the life; he that believes in me, though he were dead, yet shall he live."³² This, my brethren, is our sufficient condition under every bereaving providence, that those who sleep in Jesus, the Lord will bring with him.

Our Saviour has given us repeated proofs of his power by raising some from the dead, while (clothed in our nature) he dwelt among us. The case of Lazarus is an eminent instance, but as Lazarus and others then raised, fell victims to the stroke of death afterwards, there were not adequate assurances of our resurrection to immortal life.

In order, therefore, to lay a foundation for our liveliest hope, the Redeemer himself submitted to the abasement of death; and having remained a sufficient time under its dominion to prove that he was really dead, he arose by his own almighty power, agreeable to his former express declaration. He burst the fetters of the grave, he resumed his former appearance, and he conversed frequently with those who had been most intimate with him before his crucifixion. He convinced the most incredulous of his disciples that he was the same Jesus on whose person and instructions he had attended, thereby producing a public acknowledgment of his divinity and messiahship. After forty days, he openly ascended where he was before, directing his attendants in their future conduct, and predicting some remarkable events whereby the prevalence of his intercession might be demonstrated.

On the day of Pentecost, he imparted his promised gifts to his disciples, and the Holy Spirit bore public attestation to the truth of his doctrine and his actual government of the church. His fol-

---

[31] John 11:21.
[32] John 11:25.

lowers, satisfied of his authority, went forth preaching (among other things) the grand doctrine of the resurrection—a doctrine which constantly influenced that which they lived and taught, and in defence of which, having witnessed its success, they cheerfully suffered and died, rejoicing in hope of the glory of God. They were persuaded that because Christ lived, they should live also.

Let a firm persuasion of the truth of this doctrine reconcile our minds to the providence which has removed our deceased friend. Let us assure ourselves that he who has conquered death will redeem him from its power. Though his body shall sleep in the ground till the resurrection morning dawn, we are told that the Lord shall descend from heaven with a shout, with the voice of the archangel, and the trump of God.[33]

The trumpet, that life-giving sound, shall awake his sleeping dust and shall, quickened by the power of God, shake off the robes of mortality. His body, now in a state of corruption, shall be fashioned like to Christ's own glorious body and, arrayed in garments of immortality, will meet his coming Lord in the air. On him his Lord shall smile and bestow a crown, even a crown of righteousness, which fades not away. His happy spirit now joins the myriads of kindred spirits of just men made perfect in contemplating the mysterious glories of the incarnate God and participating of the pleasures which flow from the eternal throne. But when that period arrives, which may be termed the grand prophecy of the gospel, the members of his immortal body shall join the powers of his seraphic mind in mutual congratulations and combined gratitude.

O happy day! How pregnant are you with all our largest wishes—perfect knowledge, perfect purity, perfect and eternal felicity!

---

[33] 1 Thessalonians 4:16.

O happy day! To what society will you introduce us! All the patriarchs, prophets, apostles, martyrs, and saints of later times. There shall we meet a Watts, a Flavel, a Doddridge, a Howe, an Owen, and our friend Evans too! Now 'tis true he sleeps, and we must soon join his slumbers, but though our sleeping times differ, our waking time shall be one. In one instant all the saints of the Lord shall feel his almighty influence, and live to die no more. For, as we are planted together in the likeness of our Saviour's death, so shall we be also in the likeness of his resurrection.[34]

The resurrection opens up to us a light to cheer us amidst all the gloom of mortality. Who would be unwilling to tread the valley of the shadow of death while he believed it the path to a better and immortal life? Under all the breaches death has made, or in prospect of our own removal from our Christian friends, we are commanded to comfort one another with these words.[35]

It is our happiness also to reflect that God ever lives; that, though the channel is closed, the fountain still runs. In all ages God has provided for his church, and his name is Jehovah-Jireh still. Jesus Christ is the same yesterday, today, and forever,[36] and, by means of his own choosing, and instruments of his own preparing, he will accomplish his immutable all-wise decrees. If God had needed his servant any longer, he would not have called him from his work so soon.

Seeing how the Lord is removing his ministers from the church (and he has removed many of late), how does it behoove their hearers to give attention to their sacred message while they have them to attend upon. And how should we, who in providence are called to that important work, labour to fill up our time in our Master's service so that, whenever our Lord shall come,

---

[34] Romans 6:5.
[35] 1 Thessalonians 4:18.
[36] Hebrews 13:8.

we may be found in his employment. When we meet his approbation, we will be removed from this uncertain state to the world of uninterrupted bliss, amidst the joys of saints, the shouts of angels, and the smiles of God.

3
Christian Friendship[1]

1792

Rev and dear sir,

You request me to send you a "brief sketch of the character of my late friend and brother Mr. Josiah Evans, whilst he was at Bristol." Neither my affection for his memory, nor the pleasure I take in obliging you, will suffer me to refuse it. My acquaintance with him indeed was but of a short date, for we never saw each other till we met at the academy,[2] and he had not been there above eighteen months before the ill state of his health obliged him to leave it; since which time I have never seen him but once.

But I had not long known him before I discovered that union of good qualities in his heart which commanded my affection and respect, and distinguished him as a proper person to select for the peculiar intimacies of pious friendship. Our apartments were adjoining; we spent most of the hours of relaxation together, and in a few weeks felt a mutual attachment. I believe I had more advantages for ascertaining his real character than either of our fellow students, for he was rather of a reserved disposition, and made sure of a friend before he laid open his heart with any degree of freedom and confidence.

I found him possessed of an equitable temper of mind, seldom agitated to an undue degree at the changing scenes around him, but steadily pursuing that object to which the most mature deliberation directed him. He was not hasty indeed in determin-

---

[1] Letter to Joshua Thomas, December 21, 1792, in *The Baptist Magazine* 6 (1814): 101–105.

[2] Bristol Baptist Academy.

ing, but when he had once resolved, he was generally inflexible. Perhaps he was too positive—but it is certain that an error here is not so injurious to a student as the opposite extreme. Resolutions hastily formed are in general as hastily abandoned, and minds disposed to these sudden revolutions cannot make those advances which attend a persevering application.

Mr. J. Evans had one essential qualification for friendship, and that was faithfulness. I believe he never discerned anything in my temper or conduct which he thought would be injurious to my proficiency as a student or to my spirituality as a Christian (after our intimacy commenced), but he watched the first suitable opportunity of laying it before me with the reasons of his disapprobation. On some of these occasions he would urge his friendly admonitions and counsels with such affectionate eloquence that the result has been our retiring together with tears lamenting our mutual imperfections before God, and beseeching wisdom and grace from above to ornament our profession, and in every step to pursue something worthy of our being and character. Some of the moments we have thus spent, I believe, were marked with as true humiliation of heart as any we ever knew; for as we did not conceal the various states of our minds from each other, we had no occasion to restrain our feeling and guard our expressions in these exercises—on the contrary, we felt as much freedom as though we had not been apart, and realized the presence of none but our Maker. "A world for such a friend, to lose, is gain."

As a Christian, his views of evangelical truth were (according to my judgment) clear and consistent. His faith in them was without wavering, and the influence they had upon his heart and conduct was universal and permanent. He lived near to God. He watched over the state of his mind daily. I never found him unprepared for spiritual conversation; the things of God lay nearest his heart, and "from the abundance of the heart the mouth speaketh."³ His letters abound in good and pious sentiment. I esteem the few I have in possession as "apples of gold in baskets of silver."⁴ I never peruse them without some advantage, and by them, though dead, he yet speaks to me and helps me to converse with him.

He bid fair for great usefulness in the ministry—a strong understanding, a becoming gravity of manner, an ardent desire for usefulness, a manifest tenderness for the interests of his hearers, and manly zeal for the glory of God. A general choice of the most evangelical subjects, together with a happy talent at introducing the figurative parts of Scripture to illustrate the subjects he discoursed on, were all united in his public services. It is no wonder that he was generally acceptable to serious Christians. Nothing seemed wanting to make him eminently popular in England (for I hear he was so in Wales) but a more perfect acquaintance with the idiom of the language. Had it seemed good to the Head of the church to have continued him a few years longer, he would no doubt have filled up his deficiency, as his application was equal to his health, and his improvement to his application.

The removal of one who promised so much usefulness to the churches of God is among those mysteries of divine providence which call for the most unsuspecting confidence in the unerring wisdom and unchanging faithfulness of him who thought "he giveth no account of any of his matters"⁵ unto man, yet "doeth all things well."⁶

You, sir, are better acquainted of the particulars of my late friend's illness and decease than I am. It suffices that I have borne an honest though brief and imperfect testimony to his worth. I am happy in the confidence of your approbation from

---

³ Luke 6:45.
⁴ Proverbs 25:11.
⁵ Job 33:13.
⁶ Mark 7:37.

your personal acquaintance with this pious youth, and whilst I contemplate and admire his character, I hope I can say "*Sequor*," although I must lament that it is "*non aequis passibus.*"[7]

I am, dear sir, with affectionate respect,
Your obliged friend and junior brother,
S. Pearce.

---

[7] Referencing Virgil's *Aeneid*: "I follow, but not with equal steps."

4
Pearce's Description of Carey's Farewell[1]

1793

A letter from the Rev. Samuel Pearce, of Birmingham, to his wife, describing the actual departure of William Carey for India, on May 30, 1793.

For the sake of my own peace, I must suppose that my dearest Sarah arrived safe at her journey's end. For her sake, I trust she has experienced and expressed that gratitude to the God of all our mercies, which stamps reality and sweetness on every enjoyment of life. O that I felt more of that myself, which I cannot but recommend to my best friends. Surely, if one of God's creatures has more reason than another for praise, I am he—indulged with bodily health, mental peace, domestic comforts, providential supplies, ministerial acceptance, usefulness, with the undissembled friendship of a crowd of the people of God. Lord, who and what am I to be so distinguished? We do pray for each other, my dear Sarah, let us praise for each other, especially since we have one common interest, and the joys or griefs of one become by necessity the pleasures or pains of both.

The evening of the day you left me was distinguished by feelings of the most rapturous pleasure, wonder, and gratitude that my heart ever knew respecting the kingdom of God. Prepare, my love, to rejoice and wonder and be grateful too! I received a letter from Brother Dr. Ryland, and what do you think he wrote? Why, Carey, with all his family, are gone for India! When? How? you

---

[1] Contributed by Edward Medley, "Pearce's Description of Carey's Farewell," *Baptist Quarterly* 1.8 (October 1923): 386-387.

are ready to ask—I cheerfully satisfy you. Not long after the English fleet sailed, news came that a Danish East India Ship was to call at Great Britain in her way from Copenhagen to the East. Down came Thomas Carey to Northampton at the news last Saturday. Carey's wife (who was sufficiently recovered) offered to accompany him if her sister would go too. The sister consented, and they all set off for London together the same day. Carey wrote that Monday to Brother Ryland, saying they had found friends in London who had advances 200£ above what the society had in hand. That the sum was agreed on with the captain of the ship, and the passage of money paid down. The chaises[2] were then at the door to convey Thomas to Portsmouth, to secure the baggage left there, and to take Carey and his family to Dover, from whence they were to embark. By this time, I suppose they have sailed. If the Lord prospers them, they will get to India in time enough to receive Mrs. Thomas and the goods she has with her in the Earl of Oxford. O what a wonder working God is ours! Tell the whole now if you please, for the honor of our Great Redeemer and the encouragement of his people's faith in the most trying situations.

Three advantages are secured by the disappointment. First, the missionaries will go out more honorably, and the enemies of your cause will not have it in their power to reproach the society with publicity in transporting the missionaries under false pretenses. Second, as the Danes are a neutral power, there is no fear of their being captured by the French on their way. Thirdly, Carey has the satisfaction of his whole family, and the world have lost thereby an objection they have often raised to his going on the business.

I set off for Leicester tomorrow, and I'll go from thence to Northampton Monday or Tuesday, and most likely will ex-

---

[2] Or a light carriage.

change with Brother Ryland the following Sabbath. I entreat you will write me (on receipt of this) and account of your journey, health, friends, etc. Direct at Mr. Ryland's Northampton; if you write immediately I shall receive it before I return should I not stay a Lord's day at N.H.

All friends are well, my love to Brother and Sister Sing with the seniors and juniors of that family as well as Sister M--s and Mr. Henwood.

Do not delay writing if you have any concern for my satisfaction.

>I am, my dear dear Sarah, your own very
>Affectionate S. Pearce
>Birmingham, May 31, 1793.

5
On Doing Good[1]

1794

Since it has pleased an indulgent providence to favour us with the privilege of another interview with each other, we renew the usual token of our affectionate concern for your prosperity. It is matter of thankfulness to us that you yet exist as Christian societies, that the ordinances of God's house are continued to and enjoyed by you, and that, although some of our churches are complaining of unfruitfulness, others are in circumstances equally prosperous. It gives us pleasure, brethren, and we are persuaded that it will give you pleasure, to hear that the Lord is adding to his church of such as will be saved; but our pleasure is mingled with pain, because not all who profess have obeyed the gospel; some seemed to run well, whose progress Satan has hindered; and to preserve as far as we can the purity of our Societies, from such (according to the apostle's advice) we have withdrawn ourselves.[2] Yet, blessed be God, instances of this kind are comparatively few, and we hope they will be a useful warning to us all to "abstain from the appearance of evil," and to cry continually to God our strength, "You hold us up and we shall be safe."[3]

---

[1] This Circular Letter of the Midland Baptist Association for 1794 was signed by Pearce and the other association pastors on June 11 that year. The title has been supplied by the editor since it is simply termed "Circular Letter, 1794" in the principal source for this text, namely, William Stokes, *The History of the Midland Association of Baptist Churches, From its Rise in the Year 1655 to 1855* (London: R. Theobald/Birmingham: John W. Showell, 1855), 115–121. Transcription provided by Michael A.G. Haykin. Slight edits made.

[2] 2 Thessalonians 3:6.

[3] 1 Thessalonians 5:22; Psalm 119:117.

But, dear brethren, this is not the whole of our desire concerning you. To abstain from evil is but one trait in the Christian character; we are exhorted also to imitate our Divine Master, who went about doing good.[4] It should not satisfy us that we were once converted, that our conduct since has been irreproachable, that God is faithful, and that heaven is secure. We should be frequently reviewing what present evidences we have of piety, and be aiming at a daily growth in grace. The doctrines of sovereign mercy were never designed to cherish our indolence, nor to make us happy in a state of spiritual sloth, and to use them for this purpose is in fact to abuse them. There is not one doctrine in the gospel but what is "according to godliness,"[5] nor one promise of future happiness unconnected with present holiness. Does our Bible teach us the doctrine of God's everlasting love and his sovereign choice of his people? It declares also that they are "predestined to be conformed to the image of Christ" and "are chosen through sanctification of the Spirit, and belief of the truth."[6] Does the gospel announce the efficacious sacrifice of our blessed Redeemer on the behalf of sinners, and say, "He gave himself for us"? It is added "to redeem us from all iniquity, and to purify to himself a peculiar people zealous of good works."[7] Are we encouraged to expect the influences of the Holy Spirit? His office is to write the divine "law in our hearts and create us anew to holiness."[8] Are we comforted with the delightful doctrine of the Perseverance of the Saints? That perseverance is described by the unerring word as a "continuance in well doing."[9] Finally, is life and immortality brought to

---

[4] 1 Corinthians 11:1; Ephesians 5:1–2; 1 Peter 2:21; Acts 10:38.
[5] 1 Timothy 6:3.
[6] Romans 8:29; 2 Thessalonians 2:13.
[7] Titus 2:14.
[8] Jeremiah 31:33; Ephesians 4:24.
[9] Romans 2:7.

light by the gospel? "He that has this hope (it is said) purifies himself even as God is pure."[10]

With these considerations before us we are anxious to discover in you, brethren, not merely an abstinence from iniquity, and an adherence to the sentiments we preach (this we rejoice in), but we are concerned that you "give all diligence to add to your faith, virtue, and patience, and brotherly kindness, and charity, that you be neither barren nor unfruitful, but always abounding in the work of the Lord, pressing towards to the mark, for the prize of your high calling of God in Christ Jesus."[11] Happy shall we be, if by this address, or by any other means, we may stir you up to "forget the things which are behind, and to press after those which are before."[12]

Examine the state of your souls

To this end we beseech you first of all closely to examine into the real state of your souls. Christians should be very conversant with themselves. We hope that you have not prematurely entered on a religious profession; we trust that neither a speculative assent to the truths we maintain—a momentary transport of the passions—a fondness for the good opinion of others, nor a self-righteous dependence on the forms of religion, induced you to say, "we will go with you."[13] We entertain better hopes of you, brethren, and would take it for granted that you are Christians indeed, and that under the constraints of genuine love to Christ and his ways, you did publicly profess his name and espouse his cause.

But, dear brethren, in what state of mind are you now? Is your love any warmer, your faith any stronger, your hope more

---

[10] 1 John 3:3.
[11] 2 Peter 1:5; 1 Corinthians 15:58; Philippians 3:14.
[12] Philippians 3:13.
[13] Zechariah 8:23.

Selected Works of Samuel Pearce

vigorous, or your humility deeper than when you first knew the Lord? Or have you, amidst all the obligations of saved sinners—all the ordinances of God's house—all the promises of the gospel, and the prospects of glory, been declining in your piety? Is it possible that, as your mercies multiply, your gratitude should abate; and that while you believe the Son of God loved you with an affection which "many waters could not quench, neither the floods drown"[14] you should cool in the ardour of your affection for him? Should this be the case, hear, we beseech you, the solemn address of Christ, first to the lukewarm Ephesians, and now to you: "I have somewhat against you, because you have left your first love; remember, therefore, from where you are fallen, repent and do your first works."[15]

It will be profitable for you to examine into the causes of your declension! Have they not been irregularity in secret duties, an unnecessary association with unholy persons, too much eagerness in temporal pursuits, or the indulgence of a contentious or an unforgiving Spirit? These things, cherished or unrepented of, will as certainly injure our spirituality as strong poison without an antidote will disorder our bodies. The Spirit of God is a holy and a peaceful spirit; the indulgence of a temper or conduct dissimilar to his will grieve him and we shall be the losers. Reflect, brethren, how the degrees of our piety are connected with proportionate degrees of personal enjoyment and general usefulness. When you lived nearer to God it was better with you than now and better for all around you. Your heavenly deportment put lukewarm professors to the blush, and stirred them up to fresh ardour in religion, while "like the sun when he goes forth in his might"[16] you enlivened, encouraged, and blessed all connected with you. And what excuse can any of us make for our spiritual

---

[14] Song of Songs 8:7.
[15] Revelation 2:4–5.
[16] Judges 5:31.

On Doing Good

dullness and inactivity? Is Jesus Christ less admirable than when we first beheld his glory, or are your obligations to him less than before now? Has investigation weakened the evidences of religion, or an experimental acquaintance with the gospel lessened our sentiments of its excellency? Has God denied us a throne of mercy, or has he ceased to be gracious?

Nay, brethren, we have only ourselves to accuse, let God and his throne be blameless. Surely it becomes us to "return to the Lord—to take with us words, and say, 'O take away all iniquity, heal our backslidings, love us freely, and receive us graciously.'"[17] Heinous as our guilt has been, he still is merciful. Still he bids us come, "Return you backsliding children, and I will heal your backslidings, for I am married to you, says the Lord."[18] What gracious language! How calculated at once both to wound and heal, to convict and comfort, to reprove and to restore! To receive this address with a right spirit would be attended with deep humility and constrain us to acknowledge that all his ways are right, but ours alone are wrong, "for to us belongs shame and confusion of face, but to him belongs righteousness, because we have sinned against him."[19] With these sentiments let us look again to the cross of Christ—there we found relief at first and there alone we can obtain it now. A renewed application to Christ will produce more than regret for the past, it will stir us up to activity for the future; and indeed, that hope of mercy which leaves the soul as languid as it found it, may and ought to be suspected as counterfeit and presumptuous.

"We beseech you, therefore, by the mercies of God, that you present yourselves living sacrifices, holy, acceptable to God, which is your reasonable service."[20] Make a fresh surrender of

---

[17] Hosea 14:2, 4.
[18] Jeremiah 3:14, 22.
[19] Daniel 9:8.
[20] Romans 12:1.

yourselves to the Lord, and knowing that you are not your own property, but purchased by Immanuel's blood, strive to glorify him with "your bodies and spirits which are his."[21] Aim at obtaining an habitual sense of his omnipresence. Think and speak and act as in his sight. Watch over your spirits. Spend no idle time. Be ever doing something for God. Let no vain conversation proceed out of your mouth. Avoid foolish talking and jesting. Labour after a praying frame always, remembering that it is never well with us when we are unfit for prayer. Enter upon nothing in which you may not with propriety seek and hope to enjoy the approbation of your divine Master. Never engage in that which you are reluctant to consult God about; that reluctance proceeds from a suspicion that it is not pleasing to him, and we are told that whatever is not of faith is sin.[22] Be regular in the discharge of secret duties; why should everything in life have its stated seasons except personal religion? Think daily of our Lord's advice, "Labour not for the meat which perishes, but for that which endures to everlasting life."[23] And remember, it is in vain to call him Lord, unless we do the things he has said.[24]

Be concerned for others

But brethren, confine not your efforts to the improvement of your own hearts; be concerned for others also and endeavour to be public blessings. Have you families? Let not their blood be on your head. Converse frequently, affectionately, and seriously with your servants and children on eternal subjects. Teach them to respect the Bible. Pray with and for them. Convince them that you have their good at heart and be careful that they see nothing in your temper or conduct which you would not think becoming

---

[21] 1 Corinthians 6:20.
[22] Romans 14:23.
[23] John 6:27.
[24] Matthew 7:21.

On Doing Good

in theirs. Your advice will only be respected in proportion as it is followed with example. In your relation to the Church of Christ, be patterns to your brethren. Let your conduct as individuals be such as you think it would be right for all your fellow-members to imitate. Would it be right for all to be irregular in their attendance, to be seldom seen at social meetings for prayer, to be indifferent whether they afford pleasure to their ministers or break their hearts? If it is right for you, it is for all; but if not for all then it cannot be for you. We do most earnestly exhort you to pay the most devout attention to the instructions given by our blessed Saviour, "If your brother trespass against you ..."[25] It is highly unbecoming to neglect the Lord's Table, as some do, through a slight disagreement with a fellow-member, when they have never taken a Scriptural method to heal the breach; much worse is it to report a piece of misconduct to another before we have given the offender an opportunity for concession or repentance. Do in this, and all other cases, as you would be done by, and ever strive to deserve the characters of "The Sons of Peace."[26]

Pay attention to the state of the congregation that meets with you. Be fellow-workers with us, as we hope we are with the Lord. It is true, the characters we sustain require a more habitual devotedness to the prosperity of Zion. We are engaged by every solemn obligation to give ourselves wholly "to prayer and the ministry of the Word;"[27] but the work is great and requires the concurrence of all the friends of God. The souls of your families and of your neighbours are in some measure committed to your care. O let the perishing multitudes around you be precious in your eyes—think what Jesus Christ did to save souls and assist your Redeemer in realizing the fruit of his bloody passion and cruel death. Take every opportunity of bringing your careless

---

[25] Matthew 18:15.
[26] Matthew 5:21; Luke 10:6.
[27] Acts 6:4.

acquaintance to hear the Word of Life. And follow what we deliver in public with an affectionate personal application to their hearts. Tell them of their sad estate as guilty sinners. "Save them by plucking them out of the fire."[28] Represent to them the infinite mercy of the Lord Jesus in dying for mankind. Inform them of the guilt of neglecting his salvation, and the happiness which attends a full surrender of the heart to Christ. You, dear brethren, have "known the terrors of the Lord"[29] and have "tasted also that he is gracious."[30]

A recollection of your own feelings will give an eloquence and energy to your conversation, which, with the divine blessing, is likely above all things to affect the heart. O, if all the members of our churches were but to do all they might for God, what glorious days might we expect to see! You remember it is said in the latter day that "many shall run to and fro and knowledge shall be increased."[31] What is this but a prediction of the pious and successful activity of real Christians to promote the cause of the dear Redeemer in the world. If you are but stirred up to this activity, the prophecy will begin to be accomplished—the captivity of Zion will be drawing to an end, and Israel shall rejoice, and Judah shall be glad. Should the Lord smile on your efforts and make each of you useful to the recovery of one sinner from the error of his ways, who can tell but he also in his turn may be useful to others—and they to others—for ages yet to come, and so you may be channels through which the blessings of salvation will flow to thousands to the end of time. It may assist your determination to aim at promoting the salvation of men to look back to your unconverted state. Perhaps, awful thought, you may have been the means of provoking some to sin and so have been

---

[28] Jude 1:23.
[29] 2 Corinthians 5:11.
[30] 1 Peter 2:3.
[31] Daniel 12:4.

instrumental to their everlasting perdition; and will you be less zealous in the cause of Christ than you were in the cause of Satan?

Let not shame or the fear of displeasing men withhold you from an attempt to lead sinners to Christ. They are not ashamed of their master and his cause, why should you be ashamed of yours? They are not backward to displease God in doing evil, why should you (through fear of displeasing men) be backward to do good? They spend their time in destroying their souls and the souls of others; why should you grudge a little time to save them? You may plead that you have not much understanding and know but little. If you are Christians, you know Christ and him crucified. We only exhort you to tell them what you do know. You would warn them if you saw their bodies in danger, why not when their souls (so much more precious) are on the point of ruin? Are you apprehensive they won't hear you? If "Israel be not gathered, yet shall you have your reward."[32] Jesus Christ had not much success in his personal ministry, yet he was not discouraged. He still persevered until "he brought forth judgment unto victory."[33] Have you but little time? It ought to be filled up the better. "Whatsoever your hands find to do for God, do it with all your might."[34] What reflections will afford you the most pleasure in a dying hour: that your light has been put under a bushel or that it was placed upon a candlestick? Dear brethren, view this subject as you will view it at that solemn period. Where is the man who, in prospect of eternity, lamented that he had done too much for God? Thousands have wept because they had not done enough for him. Finally, think what pleasure it will give you at the judgment day to meet and spend eternity with some to whose salvation you have been instrumental; such a circum-

---

[32] Romans 11:7.
[33] Matthew 12:20.
[34] Ecclesiastes 9:10; Colossians 3:23.

stance would add fresh energy to your joy and lustre to your crown.

Nor should your immediate neighbours only possess your affection or engage your endeavours. A Christian's heart ought to be as comprehensive as the universe. The Asiatic, the American, and the African, as well as the European, have a claim on your philanthropy. Made of one blood, derived from one common ancestor, they are yet your brethren. Oceans and continents, though they forbid personal intercourse, do not make the relationship wider or the obligation less. In heaven you expect to join with happy spirits from every nation, kindred, and tongue under heaven. Present difference in clime, or in colour, will form no distinctions there. "All souls are equal says the Lord,"[35] and it is enough that a soul exists for a good man to use prayers and exertions for his salvation. Means are connected with ends, and when God, in his providence, gives being to the one, we may reasonably expect the other is at hand. Means are now using by our denomination as well as others to propagate the gospel among the heathen. We call you to "the help of the Lord against the mighty."[36] Has God given you the spirit of prayer? Forget not the ignorant and idolatrous, nor the men of God who are gone to show them the way of salvation.

God has freely given you food and raiment for these twenty, forty, or sixty years, have you nothing to give to him who has given all to you? Nothing for him who became poor and shed his precious blood for you? Nothing for him who has promised heaven to you? Did Christ think souls so valuable that he laid down his life for their ransom, and are they to you so insignificant that you cannot part with the superfluities of life for their sake? Can you bear to bestow that on fine clothes, or fine houses,

---

[35] Ezekiel 18:4.
[36] Judges 5:23.

or sumptuous entertainments which might maintain a servant of Christ among the heathen? O, beloved, "if there be any consolation in Christ, if any bowels of mercy, fulfill our joy,"[37] and rather deny yourselves than deny poor sinners the means of obtaining to a knowledge of the Saviour. Consider what blessings you enjoy by the gospel! Did that man of God sacrifice too much who brought the news of a Redeemer first to England? And can you sacrifice too much to send those transporting tidings to Asia or Africa? God will fulfill his own Word and give "the uttermost parts of the earth to his Son for his possession."[38] Let your love to Christ decide whether you shall be helpers in this glorious cause or not.

Brethren, we live in an eventful age; nature appears almost in convulsions—kingdom rises up against kingdom, and nation against nation; these are signs of the times and forewarn us that "the end of all things is hand."[39] "Watch, therefore, as those who wait for the Lord."[40] Have as little as possible to do with the world. Meddle not with political controversies, an inordinate pursuit of these (we are sorry to observe) have been as canker-worms at the root of vital piety, and caused "the love of many" (formerly zealous professors) "to wax cold."[41] The Lord reigns! 'Tis our place to rejoice in his government, and "quietly to wait for the salvation of God."[42] The establishment of his kingdom will be the ultimate of all those national commotions which now terrify the earth.[43] "The wrath of man shall praise him, and the remainder of wrath he will restrain."[44] Attentive

---

[37] Philippians 2:1.
[38] Psalms 2:8.
[39] Matthew 24:6-7; Mark 13:8; 1 Peter 4:7.
[40] Matthew 24:42; Mark 13:35; Luke 12:35.
[41] Matthew 24:12.
[42] Lamentations 3:26.
[43] Revelation 19:15.
[44] Psalm 76:10. Pearce had preached on this passage just over a month before he wrote this circular letter.

Christians may hear their Saviour's voice amidst all these desolating scenes, "Behold! I come quickly."[45] Happy for those who can confidently reply, "Amen, even so, come, Lord Jesus."[46]

Finally, brethren, farewell. Be of good comfort. Be of one mind. Live in love, and the God of love and peace shall be with you.

---

[45] Revelation 22:7, 12.
[46] Revelation 22:20.

6
The Scripture Doctrine of Christian Baptism[1]

1794

To the Church of Christ,
Assembling for divine worship in Harvey Lane Leicester

My dear friends,

The following discourse, which you have already heard from the pulpit, I now submit to your private inspection. Should the perusal tend to revive in your hearts the sacred pleasures of that solemn day on which it was delivered, or to increase the numbers of those, who like our divine Lord are desirous of "fulfilling all righteousness,"[2] I shall not regret my compliance with your entreaties for its publication. But we have never more need of watchfulness over the frame of our spirits than when we are engaged in religious controversies, lest in the spirit of contest we lose the spirit of meekness and of love. Victory too often makes us vain, and impotence in argument inflames the zeal it should annihilate. Perhaps no controverted point has more frequently occasioned an undue exercise of the passions than the subject of the ensuing sermon. Suffer me therefore, my Christian Brethren, affectionately to caution you against an unbecoming triumph in the prevalence of the sentiments you espouse, or any uncharitable censures on those whose opinions and practice differ from your own. The same volume in which we are exhorted to "Stand

---

[1] *The Scripture Doctrine of Christian Baptism with some historical remarks on that subject* (Birmingham/New York, 1825).
[2] Matthew 3:15.

fast in the faith, to quit ourselves like men, and be strong,"[3] contains also numerous injunctions to forbearance and charity. We never afford any real service to our divine Master by contending for his cause if it is not in his spirit. Nothing will so effectually recommend the truth as the distinguished amiableness of those who profess it. Let the same mind, therefore, be in you which was in Christ Jesus; the character he sustained you cannot contemplate without admiring. He was "meek and lowly of heart;" imbibe his spirit and you will "find rest for your souls."[4]

It will be singular if you are not opposed in proportion to your prosperity. Be not surprised if that opposition comes from those of whose piety, in other respects, you entertain the most respectful sentiments; "To err is human." Indulge not an angry thought on such occasions; neither return railing for railing,[5] but rather imitate him, "who when he was reviled, reviled not again;"[6] and overcome evil with good.

I am persuaded, my brethren, that you will never seek an increase of your number, or the propagation of your sentiments by secret and disingenuous efforts; methods as frequently, though undeservedly, imputed to our denomination. Rather let us ever have it in our power to say with the Lord, "I spoke openly to the world; I have taught in the Synagogue and the temple where the people resort, and in secret I have said nothing" (John 18:20).

But suffer not any difference of opinion on the positive institutions of our religion, to interrupt your fellowship with other Christians as long as it may be cultivated to mutual edification. Remember that you have all one centre of union—Christ Jesus, and you expect to meet with millions in heaven who are distinguished by different names on earth. Charity must teach you to

---

[3] 1 Corinthians 16:13.
[4] Matthew 11:29.
[5] 1 Peter 3:9.
[6] 1 Peter 2:23.

Baptism

think as highly of their sincerity as you expect justice should teach them to think of yours—we have a right to form a judgement on the actions of men, but it is God's prerogative to search the heart.[7] And so it ill becomes us to judge any man to be a hypocrite because he does not see with our eyes.

It would occasion real grief, were I to imagine that anything contained in the following pages was calculated to promote a different spirit from what I have now recommended to you. If I knew of such a paragraph I would expunge it, as a disgrace to myself and an injury to the cause I espouse. Happy in my extensive acquaintance with ministers, and other Christians of different persuasions, I would carefully avoid the use of any language which a candid opponent would condemn. I should have been glad had my time (when the following discourse was delivered) permitted me to have been more copious in a practical improvement of the subject. As a valuable substitute, I beg leave to recommend to you an excellent little tract, written by Mr. Foot, entitled *A Practical Discourse Concerning Baptism*;[8] a book which would be profitable pocket-companion for every pious Baptist.

I have only now, brethren, to congratulate you on the kind appearance of the great Head of the church on your behalf, since providence has removed your late worthy pastor to so distant, and in some respects, so different a scene of action.

Your generous acquiescence in the removal of a man you so deservedly esteemed has not been forgotten by him whose cause you have made this sacrifice to promote. Regard, my brethren, your recent prosperity as a proof of your divine Saviour's approbation, and be encouraged cheerfully to make any future sacrifice to which providence may call you. Thus, while our dear

---

[7] Jeremiah 17:10.
[8] William Foot, *A Practical Discourse Concerning Baptism* (London: Aaron Ward, 1739).

brother and his colleague are serving God in Asia, let us employ ourselves in Europe,

> looking for the blessed hope, and the glorious appearing of the great God and our Saviour Jesus Christ, who gave himself for us, that he might redeem us from all iniquity, and purify to himself a peculiar people zealous of good works.[9]

I am, my dear friends,
Your willing servant in the Gospel of Christ,

Samuel Pearce
Birmingham, May 20, 1794.

---

[9] Titus 2:13-14.

The Doctrine of Christian Baptism

"But we desire to hear of you what you think; for as concerning this sect, we know that everywhere it is spoken against."
Acts 28:22

These words were addressed to the apostle Paul, by some of the principal Jews in Rome, when he was sent from Jerusalem a prisoner to that city. Though it is uncertain at what period or by what means the gospel was first published in the metropolis of the Roman Empire, it is evident that at this time some Christians resided there. These Paul addressed by letter three years before he saw them, and though coming in chains, he was affectionately met by some of them above fifty miles from the city. Yet, whether owing to the smallness of their number, their voluntary concealment, or the general contempt in which they were held, it appears they were as little noticed by the Roman Jews as by the Roman Pagans. But the zealous apostle, ever active in his Master's service, was unwilling that his countrymen should be any longer ignorant of him "whom to know is eternal life."[10] We are informed, therefore, that after three days, he invited the chief of the Jews to a friendly conference[11] wherein he relates to them the unjust treatment he had received from his own nation and assures them that his appeal to Caesar was made not with a design to impeach his enemies, but for his personal security. He then declares that his present confinement was for the testimony he bore to the Messiah, the common object of hope to all the posterity to Abraham.

---

[10] John 17:3.
[11] Acts 28:17.

To this they reply, that neither by letters nor word of mouth had they been informed of anything to his prejudice—that indeed the sect, of which he was a teacher, was universally reproached;[12] yet that they were willing, yea desirous, to hear what he had to say in vindication of himself and his doctrines. The temper and conduct of these Jews merit universal imitation. They acted on maxims which reflection and experience fully justified, such as that popularity is no certain standard of truth; and that impartial investigation ought always to precede a final decision. On these principles let us act today.

I feel myself this morning in some respects circumstanced like the apostle to the Gentiles. I appear a teacher of a sect almost everywhere spoken against, not only in private circles but in public assemblies; not only by the profane but by the professor; a sect whose members have been anathematized in councils. I am in one part of the world drowned, burnt in another, and everywhere opposed. I stand today before many who differ from me in opinion, yet are desirous to hear what I can advance in support of my sentiments and practice. It is with pleasure I meet such an assembly, and hope to find as much candour among professed Christians at Leicester as Paul found among the Jews at Rome. I cheerfully enter on the service to which the providence of God and your expectations call me.

The question before us, my brethren, is not respecting the truth of Christianity; here we are all united, and with one heart subscribe the address of Peter to his Saviour: "We believe and are sure that you are the Christ the Son of the living God" (John 6:69). Nor are we (I presume) divided on the fundamental truths

---

[12] The ancients say that the Jews at Jerusalem sent distinguished men over all the world, in order to represent the Christians as a set of Atheists, and guilty of the foulest crimes. See the Latin of Origen, *Contra Celsum*, 6.40.

Justin Martyr also charges the Jews with sending select persons all over the world for this purpose (selectos viros in universam terram emisistis). In Eusebius, *Church History*, 4.18.7.

Baptism

of our holy religion. We all believe that there is a day appointed in which God will judge the world in righteousness.[13] We believe that as sinners we are all liable to his endless displeasure, and that there is no way of deliverance from the wrath to come, but through faith in Jesus Christ our Lord—without holiness no man can see God.[14]

We agree further that Jesus is the supreme governor of his Church; that his revealed will is the only rule of Christian duty; and that it would be an insult to his dignity to advance the traditions of men above his commandments, or even on a level with them.

The point in question is: "What is the mind and will of Christ?" We all wish to please him, but what would he have us do? Here we differ, at least in one subject, and that is baptism. Some of us believe that Jesus has limited the ordinance to persons professing faith and repentance; and that the primitive and Scriptural way of administering it is by the immersion of the whole body in the water in the name of the Father, Son, and Holy Spirit. But others present imagine that the infant offspring of professing Christians have an equal right to baptism with believers; and that the application of water by pouring or sprinkling is valid baptism. With the former I unite, and their views I will endeavour to defend by assigning our reasons:

1. For administering baptism by immersion only.
2. For confining this ordinance to those who make a personal profession of faith and repentance.

But before I enter on discussion of the points, it is needful we should agree on some rule of judgement which, being on both

---

[13] Acts 17:31.
[14] Hebrews 12:14.

sides acknowledged determinate, will supersede the necessity of all farther appeal. This rule is laid down by the prophet Isaiah: "To the law and to the testimony; if they speak not according to these, it is because there is no light in them."[15] To suppose the Scriptures inadequate to the instruction of man is to impeach both the wisdom and justice of their author; and the two following maxims formed on the sufficiency of Scripture in matters of religion, appear to be not only safe, but necessary to those who take part with the great Chillingworth and say, "The Bible, the Bible is the Religion of Protestants."[16]

1. Nothing is or can be a part of Christian worship which is not recommended either by precept or example in the holy Scriptures.
2. It is a sin against God to live in the neglect of that which we find recommended to us in his Word.

I will close this observation in the words of Dr. Owen, who says:

> The main of the Church's chaste and choice affection to Christ, lies in their keeping his institution and his worship, according to his appointment. The breach of this he calls Adultery and Whoredom everywhere. On this account those believers who really attend to communion with Jesus Christ will receive nothing in his worship but what is of his appointment.[17]

---

[15] Isaiah 8:20.
[16] William Chillingworth, *The Religion of Protestants: A Safe Way to Salvation* (London: 1846), 463.
[17] John Owen, *On Communion with God*, vol. 2 in *The Works of John Owen*, ed. William H. Goold (Philadelphia: Leighton Publications, 1862), 150.

Why immersion is essential to baptism

In these remarks, I hope we are agreed and, on these principles, I proceed to declare why we believe immersion essential to baptism.

The meaning of baptism: immersion
First, because to immerse is the primary meaning of the word employed by Christ to express the act of baptism; and therefore, while a partial application of water (be it by pouring or sprinkling) bears the name of baptism, it cannot be the thing. It should be remarked that the Greek word is not translated into the English tongue, but is adopted from the Greek to the English Testament, and it is this circumstance which confound the judgment of common readers. Were the word to be actually translated, no man would dare to make our Lord's commission run thus, "Go teach all nations, sprinkling them—or he that believes and is sprinkled, or has water poured upon him shall be saved." But whether it would be wrong to translate the word immerse, and say, "Go teach the nations, *immersing* them."[18] let the following considerations determine,

1. The word (βάπτω and its derivative βαπτιζω) is thus rendered from the Septuagint translation of the Old Testament, and also from the New.[19] See 2 Kings 5:14. Naaman (εβαπτισατο) dipped himself; John 8:26 (βαψας) I have dipped; Luke 16:24 (βαψη) he may dip; and also Revelation 19:13 (βεβαμμενον)

---

[18] Matthew 28:19.
[19] It is acknowledged that the word is not always *translated* dipping; but it may be asserted that it is never used in the Bible to express anything short of the total covering, or universal application. To justify this remark, let that prodigy of learning, Professor Venema, give his opinion. "The word, ... to baptize, is nowhere used in the Scripture for sprinkling—no, not in Mark 7:4." Abraham Booth, *Paedobaptism Examined, on the Principles, Concessions, and Reasonings, of the Most Learned Paedobaptists. A Reply to "A Treatise on Baptism," by Matthew Henry* (London, 1787), 1:54.

dipped in blood, etc. If it means dipping in one place, why not in another?

2. In the German, Dutch, and Danish Testaments, where the word is translated, it is rendered by words signifying to dip. In German, *teuff*; in Dutch, *doop*; in Danish, *dobe*; and John the Baptist, with them, goes by the name of John the Dipper.[20]

3. The most eminent divines and critics of all persuasions, even among the Paedobaptists, have acknowledged that the word our Lord uses means to dip or immerse. Above eighty such testimonies have been collected and given to the world: among which are the evidences of Calvin and Luther, with many English divines both among the Episcopalians and Dissenters.[21] Are all these in league to plead falsely against their own practice?

4. But what seems most incontestably to prove that to baptize means to dip is the practice of the Greek Church, whose members, reading the New Testament in its original and their maternal tongue, must certainly be better qualified to judge concerning the meaning of a term than foreigners; and they have uniformly, from the apostles' time to this day, practiced Baptism by immersion.[22]

---

[20] "'What is Christian dipping?' Answer: Water, in conjunction with the word, and command of Christ. 'What is implied in the command, Matthew 28:19; Mark 16:15-16?' Answer: A command to the dipper and the dipped, with the promise of Salvation to those who believe. 'How is this Christian dipping to be administered?' Answer: The person must be deep dipped in water, or overwhelmed with it in the name of God the Father, &c." Danish Catechism, in Abraham Booth's *Paedobaptism Examined*, 1:46-47.

[21] Abraham Booth, *Paedobaptism Examined*, 1:308.

[22] See Thomas Smith, *An Account of the Greek-Church: As to Its Doctrine and Rites of Worship with Several Historical Remarks Interspersed, Relating Thereunto. To Which Is Added, an Account of the State of the Greek Church, under Cyrillus Lucaris Patriarch of Constantinople, with a Relation of His Sufferings and Death* (London, 1680), 112; and John G. King, *The Rites and Ceremonies of the Greek Church in Russia: Containing an Account of Its Doctrine, Worship, and Discipline* (London, 1772), 192.

Baptism

The phraseology of baptism

Secondly, we justify immersion not only from the plain meaning of the word used in the command, but also from the phraseology used in the accounts given us of primitive baptism. Thus, "they were baptized of him in Jordan" (Matt. 3:6), so it is said of our Lord's baptism, "He was baptized of John in Jordan" (Mark 1:5).[23] and to this well agrees the account which Matthew gives of what followed, "And Jesus, when he was baptized, went up straightway out of the water" (Matt. 3:16).

The same language is employed in the Acts of the Apostles. In the close of the eighth chapter, we have a narrative of the conversion and baptism of an Ethiopian eunuch by the Evangelist Philip. In Acts 8:36, we read they came to a certain water; they went down both into the water, and Philip baptized him (8:36); and we are told they came up out of the water (8:39). Let us divest ourselves of all pre-conceptions, and suppose we were hearing an account of a ceremony in which we had no concern. Let the passages I have referred you to, be repeated, and who among you would ever think that the ceremony described was performed by sprinkling or pouring? Or suppose yourselves relating the Christian rite of baptism to a stranger, who understood neither the Greek, Latin, French, nor any language with which the word baptize was incorporated—what word in that stranger's language would you employ to express the act of baptizing? Would you say "Jesus was sprinkled of John in Jordan" or "Jesus was poured of John in Jordan"? Would this be intelli-

---

[23] As it is more than probable that some attentive readers of the Scriptural accounts of baptism may conceive that the force of this argument is weakened by the use of the preposition "with" in other verses of the chapters here referred to, as Matthew 3:11, "I baptize you with water..." it is necessary to remark, that in Greek the same preposition (εν) is used by the uninspired writers, though differently rendered by the translators—that this preposition is rendered "in" on other occasions, as Matthew 8:32, (απεθανον εν τοισ υδασιν) "perished in the waters"—Luke 3:20 (εν τη φυλακη) "in prison"—that in is the primary sense of that preposition, and that it is so rendered in the Vulgate Latin, followed by Montanus.

gible language? But to say he was "immersed" in Jordan would be good sense and sound theology.

The location of baptism
Thirdly, that immersion was the primitive practice, appears also from the places which were chosen for the purpose of baptizing: the Jordan, a large river; "and Enon, near Salim, because there was much water there" (John 3:23).[24]

The representation of baptism
Fourth, the representation which is given of baptism in the New Testament can agree only with the act of immersion. The Apostle Paul, in his Epistles both to the Romans and Colossians[25] compares it to a burial, which every child knows is the covering of the body entirely, not casting a few particles of earth upon it. Dr. Whitby says, "It is expressly declared in these passages, 'that we are buried with Christ in Baptism, by being buried under water;'"[26] and the change of this mode into sprinkling, he

---

[24] "Since sprinkling came into fashion, criticism unheard of in former ages, has endeavoured to derive evidence for scarcity of water from the Greek text of the Evangelist John, and to render (πολλα υδατα) not 'much water,' but 'many waters.' It is observable, that the rivers Euphrates at Babylon, Tiber at Rome, and Jordan in Palestine, are all described by (πολλα υδατα) (Jeremiah 51:13; Revelation 17:1; 18; and Ezekiel 19) compared with Numbers 24:7 (alluding to the lions that lay in the thickets of Jordan). The thunder which agitates clouds charged with floods is called the voice of the Lord upon many waters; and the attachment that no mortification can annihilate is a love which many waters cannot quench, neither can the floods drown (Psalm 29:3; Song of Songs 8:7). How it came to pass that a mode of speaking, which on every occasion signifies much, should in the case of baptism signify little, is a question not easy to answer." Robert Robinson, *The History of Baptism* (Boston: 1817), 26. Also the sound of the united and loud praises of all the inhabitants of heaven, which is compared to the voice of a great thunder, is said to have been like the voice of many waters (φωνην υδατα πολλων) in Revelation 14:2.

[25] Romans 6:4; Colossians 2:12.

[26] Pearce also makes note of lecture 202, "Of the Mode of Baptism," from Philip Doddridge, *The Works of the Rev. P. Doddridge, D.D.*, vol. 5 (Leeds: Edward, Baines, 1804), 323–324. See Daniel Whitby, *A Paraphrase and Commentary on the New Testament*, vol. 2 (London: Awnsham and John Churchill, 1703), 31. Annotation for Romans 6:4.

confesses, was without any allowance from the Author of the institution.[27] This witness is true; but if Jesus Christ never gave allowance, where do we derive authority to alter his laws? Are we not giving him occasion to complain that we have made void his commandments by our traditions? And can it be pleasing in his sight for the disciple to exalt himself above his Lord?

The history of baptism

The introduction of this mode of baptizing was gradual; the pretenses for it were plausible; and as it made its way in proportion to the ignorance of the times, we need not wonder at it becoming general in the fourteenth century.

In all ages, mankind has discovered a strong attachment to the ceremonials of their religion, and the Eastern Church is to this day a miserable proof how ceremonies may continue when real religion has taken its flight. Our Savior, who well knew this propensity of human nature, has avoided introducing a multitude of ceremonies into his spiritual dispensation—two only he appointed, and the folly of his professed disciples in relation to these two, manifests his wisdom in instituting no more. Baptism, which at first was designed as a public acknowledgment of Christianity, soon began to be regarded as essential not only to a public profession of Christ, but also to an interest in the blessing of his salvation.

Hence, when persons who had not been baptized were taken ill, and apprehended death, they became anxious lest, for want of baptism, they should lose their souls. Nobody would think it prudent to put a dying man into a cold bath, and yet everybody wished the Christian to be perfected by baptism.[28] It was

---

[27] Whitby, *Paraphrase and Commentary*, 31. Annotation for Romans 6:4.

[28] Basil, inviting the young people of his Congregation to be baptized, asks, "when will you be made a Christian?" intimating that baptism was necessary to Christianity itself.

thought more remarkable for its ingenuity than piety, that water might be brought to him who would not be brought under water; and the earliest account we have of clinic baptism is in the case of Novation in the third century.[29] Cyprian, bishop of Carthage, is the first among the ancients whose writings plead for this practice. About the year 255, one Magnus writes to know his opinion of it. His answer would satisfy every candid mind, that he approved the practice, not because he found it authorized by Jesus Christ, but because, to use his own words:

> He did, according to the best of his mean capacity, judge, that divine favours are not capable of diminution or injury, nor did he imagine anything less than the full blessing could be enjoyed, where the divine bounty is received with a full and perfect faith, both of the giver and receiver.[30]

Approved by a Bishop, no wonder if in all cases of necessity, the practice was continued in Africa as long as the ecclesiastical order had influence there. But it was not till the year 754 that sprinkling received a public toleration in Europe, obtained from Pope Steven III who, having fled for security from the Lombards to Pepin, King of France, some Monks of Cressy, in Brittany, took the opportunity of asking the opinion of his Holiness on nineteen questions, and among them they proposed this: "whether in cases of necessity, it was not lawful to baptize by

---

[29] The account of Novation's affusion is given by Eusebius in the following words: "He fell into a severe sickness, and as he seemed as he was about to die, he received baptism by affusion, on the bed whereon he lay; if indeed we can say that such a one did receive it." Eusebius, *Church History*, 6.43.14–15.

[30] "Nos, quantum concipit mediocritas nostra, aestimamus in nullo mutilari et debilitari posse beneficia divina, nec minus aliquid illic posse contingere, ubi plena et tota fide et dantis et sumentis accipitur, quod de divinis muneribus hauritur." Epist. *Ad Magnum*, 9. Pearce here translates the above Latin quotation: "He fell dangerously ill, and being, as it was thought, at the point of death, he received the infusion of Baptism on the bed whereon he lay, if that may be termed a Baptism."

Baptism

pouring water from the hand or a cup."[31] To which the Pontiff replied that in such a case of necessity such a baptism should be valid. This was a considerable step towards the universal practice of pouring, or aspersion; yet it was 557 years after this, in 1311, that a council at Ravenna declared sprinkling or dipping indifferent. Till now sprinkling was a thing so rare that Dr. Whitby scruples not to say, "immersion was religiously observed by all Christians for 13 Centuries;"[32] and indeed after this time, for two or three Centuries, it appears to have prevailed in Europe.

Erasmus, who lived in England part of Henry VIII's reign, testifies that then baptism was administered in England by dipping.[33] In the following reign (Edward VI) the Common Prayer Book enjoins dipping, unless in case of weakness. In the reign of Mary, no material alteration appears to have taken place in the mode of administering baptism; but in the following, a very considerable advance was made in the present universal practice of the English Episcopal Clergy, "so that, in the later times of Queen Elizabeth,[34] and during the reigns of King James, and King Charles I, very few children were dipped in the font."

During the Commonwealth, the primitive practice was almost excluded. When the directory for public worship was forming in the assembly of Divines at Westminster, the question was agitated, whether dipping should be excluded or retained? Dr. Lightfoot strenuously contended for its conclusion; and

---

[31] The Synod of Aix, held in AD 1583, improved on this idea, and ordered that the pouring of the water should be performed with a ladle, kept in the font for that purpose. See William Wall, *History of Infant Baptism* (London, 1707), 468.

[32] Daniel Whitby, commentary on Romans 6:4.

[33] Wall, *History of Infant Baptism*, 467.

[34] The latitude (says Dr. Wall) given in the Liturgy, which could have but little effect in the short reign of Edward, might, during the long reign of this Queen (Elizabeth) produce an alteration proportionately greater. It being allowed to weak children (though strong enough to be brought to church) to be baptized by affusion, many fond ladies and gentlewomen first, and then by degrees the common people, would obtain the favour of the Priest to have their children pass for weak children, too tender to endure dipping in the water. Wall, *History of Infant Baptism*, 470.

though the doctor carried his point, it was but by a single vote, there being 25 against 24 and the decision of the assembly was established by an ordinance of Parliament,[35] in 1644. At the restoration, the *Common Prayer Book* used in former reigns was reviewed, and the Rubric thrown into the form in which it now stands; whereby dipping is recognized as the proper mode, but affusion is allowed in case of weakness.

It is not unworthy of remark that in those countries only where the Pope has established his anti-Christian throne, the rite has been changed from dipping to aspersion. In all other Christian countries, and among all the Eastern Christians, the institution is preserved in its original form and baptism is still administered by immersion.

On the whole it appears that the appreciating of inward religion at too low a rate, and the exterior of Christianity too highly,[36] gave birth to that general departure from the apostolic mode of baptizing, which we now lament and wish if possible to reform.

Persons professing faith and repentance

Time calls our attention to the other part of my design, and I proceed to justify the limitation of this ordinance to persons professing faith and repentance.

The chief grounds of our conduct are these: First, we can find no divine command for baptizing any other subjects. Second, the

---

[35] The Directory orders, that "as the minister pronounces the words, 'I baptize thee, &c.' he shall baptize the child with water, which for the manner of doing it, is not only lawful but sufficient, and most expedient to be by pouring or sprinkling water on the face of the child, without adding any other ceremony." See Chapter 14.1 of the *Book of Common Prayer*.

[36] Baptism has been deemed so absolutely necessary to salvation that when no water has been near it has been administered with sand; at other times it has been given to the dead; and frequently the genius of the compassionate has been exercised in devising means for baptizing unborn babes, whose lives might be thought endangered in their delivery. See Abraham Booth, *Paedobaptism Examined* (London: 1829) 3:221–222. See also Robinson, *History of Baptism*, 433.

Bible does not afford examples of any other persons receiving baptism. Thirdly, we conceive that the great end for which baptism was appointed can be answered in no other subjects whatever.

No command for baptizing any other subjects
The sole authority which Christian ministers have for baptizing at all is the commission given by our Lord after his resurrection, which is recorded by two Evangelists. In Matthew 28:19-20, it reads: "Go therefore, and teach all nations, baptizing them in the name of the Father, and of the Son, and of the Holy Spirit; teaching them to observe all things whatever I have commanded you." I cannot conceive of a more accurate comment on this text, than has been already given by the pious Mr. Baxter, whose words are these:

> This is not like some occasional historical mention of baptism, but it is the very commission of Christ to his Apostles for preaching and baptizing, and purposely expresses their several works in their several places and order. Their first task is by teaching, to make disciples; the second work is to baptize them; the third work is to teach them all other things which are afterwards to be learned in the school of Christ. To contemn this order, is to renounce all rules of order; for where can we expect to find it, if not here.[37]

The same commission is thus repeated by Mark: "Go into all the world and preach the Gospel to every creature, he that believes and is baptized shall be saved, but he that believes not shall be damned" (Mark 16:15-16). Here we have the propagation and

---

[37] Richard Baxter, *Certain Disputations of Right to Sacraments, and the True Nature of Visible Christianity; Defending Them against the Second Assault of That Pious, Reverend and Dear Brother Mr. Thomas Blake* (London, 1658), 148-149. Pearce references this from Booth, *Paedobaptism Examined*, 7:270.

influence of Christianity described in its various parts: 1. Preaching the Gospel, 2. Believing the Gospel, 3. Baptism on profession of that faith, and 4. Salvation as promised to all baptized believers. Accordingly, Doddridge thus paraphrases the 16th verse:

> I now solemnly declare, that he who sincerely believes your testimony, and in token of that cordial faith is baptized in my name, and continues to maintain a temper and conduct suitable to that engagement, shall certainly be saved.[38]

Now as these two passages are our only authorities for baptizing at all, and as neither of them commands the baptizing of any besides those who are discipled to Christianity, we should deem it unwarrantable presumption to baptize any other, and expect a reproof similar to that which God gave the children of Israel by the prophet Isaiah:

> Bring no more vain oblations, your calling of assemblies I cannot away with; it is iniquity, even the solemn meeting. When you come to appear before me, who has required this at your hands? (Isa. 1:12–13).

No biblical examples of any other persons receiving baptism
Had the practice of the apostles given a sanction to the baptism of infants, we should certainly (regarding their conduct as the best exposition of our Lord's meaning) have yielded to the authority of their example; acknowledging that those who were so plentifully endued with the Holy Spirit and were designed to lay the foundation of the Christian church, could not misinterpret

---

[38] See Philip Doddridge, *The Family Expositor: or a Paraphrase and Version of the New Testament: with Critical Notes; and a Practical Improvement of each Section*, vol. 2, 3rd ed. (London: J. Waugh and W. Fenner, 1756), 667. Comments on Mark 16:16.

Baptism

the commission they had received from the Lord; but it cannot be asserted that in any one place of the inspired apostolic history an example of infant baptism can be found. Presuming on your patience, I will recite every account which we have in the New Testament of the administration of Baptism by the apostles or their contemporaries:

1. Acts 2:41: "Then (that is, after they had been pricked in their hearts; made earnest inquiry after salvation; and been directed by Peter to penitence and baptism) they that gladly received his word were baptized."

2. Acts 8:12-13: "When they (the Samaritans) believed Philip preaching the things concerning the Kingdom of God and the name of Jesus Christ, they were baptized, both *men and women*. Then Simon himself believed also, he was baptized."

3. Acts 8:36-38: "The eunuch said, 'see here is water; what hinders me to be baptized?' And Philip said, 'If you believe with all thy heart you may.' And he answered, 'I believe that Jesus Christ is the Son of God.' And Philip baptized him."

4. Acts 9:18, compared with 22:16: "Ananias said, 'Brother Saul, the Lord Jesus has sent me that you may be filled with the Holy Spirit; and now what tarriest you? Arise and be baptized.' And he arose, and was baptized."

5. Acts 10:44-48: "While Peter spoke, the Holy Spirit fell on all who heard the Word—they spoke with tongues and magnified God. Then answered Peter, 'can any man forbid water, that these should not be baptized, who have received the Holy Spirit, as well as we? And we commanded them to be baptized."

6. Acts 16:14-15: "And a certain woman, named Lydia, a seller of purple, of the city of Thyatira, which worshipped God, heard us, whose heart the Lord opened that she attended to the things which were spoken of Paul, and she was baptized, and her household."

Further remarks concerning Lydia's household

As much has been said from the baptism of Lydia's household, in favour of infant baptism, a few remarks on the passage seem necessary.

1. There is no proof of her being a married woman, rather the contrary; for if she had a husband, it would have been most natural for him to have gone to Philippi to sell the purple, and not have sent his wife.

2. Supposing she had a husband, who can tell that she had children by him?

3. If she had had children, how do we know of what age they were, or whether they might not have died in infancy?

4. It is said that, "when the Apostles left Philippi they entered into Lydia's house, and comforted the brethren" (Acts 16:40). It is evident; therefore, her household were capable of spiritual consolation; for none but such could the Apostles give, and such, none but adults could receive.[39]

5. Thyatira (to which place Lydia belonged) was a city of Lesser Asia, near 300 miles from Philippi, the Aegean Sea lying between the two cities. Let any man judge whether, supposing Lydia to be a married woman, to have at this time children, and those children to be infants. Is it likely that she would take them from their home in Thyatira to Philippi, and expose them to the fatigues and hazard of so long a journey?

6. In the same chapter we have another account of the administration of this ordinance, "And they (Paul and Silas) spoke to the jailer the Word of the Lord, and to all that were in his

---

[39] Calvin, though a Paedobaptist, appears to have considered Lydia's household as adults, and actually converted to Christ by her means; he says, "I confess that Lydia had not the hearts of all her house at her disposal, so that she could convert them at her own pleasure to Christ; but God attended her pious efforts with his blessing, that her domestics yielded to her endeavours, or become obedient." See John Calvin, *Commentary on Galatians*, Acts 16:15.

house—and he was baptized, he and all his straightway; and he rejoiced, believing in God, with all his house" (Acts 16:32-34).

7. Take Acts 18:8, compared with 1 Corinthians 1:14: "And Crispus, the chief Ruler of the Synagogue, believing on the Lord, with all his house; and I (Paul) baptized Crispus, and Gaius (my host)[40] And many of the Corinthians, hearing, believed, and were baptized."

8. See Acts 19:1-5. It has been questioned whether the persons here spoken of were baptized both by John and Paul, or whether Paul is not, in the 5th verse, reminding them that John baptized his disciples into the faith or name of the Lord Jesus, the great Messiah, whose way he was sent to prepare. The latter opinion is the most probable; but either way it is evident that these were "twelve men," and not children.

9. The last account we have is in 1 Corinthians 1:16: "I (Paul) baptized also the household of Stephanas;" and in the 16th chapter of the same Epistle, it is said, "The house of Stephanas addicted themselves to the ministry of the saints" (1 Cor. 16:15).

Now these are all the instances of baptism administered in the Apostles' days, which I find an account of in the New Testament. It cannot be denied, that though the book of Acts includes the history of the first thirty years of the Christian church, in which time we read of the baptism of thousands; and though, on many occasions, the detail is exceedingly minute, yet there is not one instance of infant baptism throughout the whole. Therefore, how can that be considered as a necessary part of the constitution of the Christian church, which Christ never commanded, and which his inspired ministers never practiced!

---

[40] Romans 16:23.

Scriptures used for infant baptism

It is true, appeals have been made to Scripture for the support of this rite; but it is as true that the Scripture authorities to which these appeals have been generally made, are such as have no reference to baptism at all.[41] It is beside the design of this sermon to combat the arguments brought in favour of the baptism of infants; it is enough if we prove the truth of our premises and the justice of our conclusions; this done, it will invalidate every effort to justify an opposite practice; yet as there are two or three popular texts cited in favour of infant baptism, it may not be improper briefly to investigate what degree of relation they bear to the argument.

Scarcely a book is published, or a sermon preached in defense of infant baptism without reference to Matthew 19:14 and Mark 10:14-16, but is there a word about baptism in either of these accounts? Not one. On the contrary, we are first expressly told for what purpose these children were brought by their parents—so that Christ "should touch them" or that he might "put his hands on them and pray." Second, we are particularly informed what Christ did with them, "he took them up in his arms, put his hands upon them and blessed them." Third, we are assured by John "that Jesus baptized not,"[42] and if he did not baptize at all, how could he baptize these little ones?

---

[41] Dr. John Edwards (1637-1716) makes appeal to one passage of Scripture, which in his own language, "solves this great controversy with the Anabaptists."—Venerable umpire in this tedious contest, we wait impatiently thy deciding voice. Prepare ye opposers of the baptism of infants for a final overthrow! The umpire is Solomon, the wisest of mankind; and to decide the point at once, he says, 'risum teueatis amici!' (Song of Sgs: 8:2); "Thy navel is as a round goblet, which wanteth not liquor." See Booth, *Paedobaptist Examiner*, 2:416. Booth is referencing John Edwards, *Exercitations, Critical, Philosophical, Historical, Theological: On Several Important Places in the Writings of the Old and New Testament* (London: Jonathan Robinson, John Lawrence, and John Wyat, 1702), 136-137. See "On Canticles 7: 2." Patrick suggests the same thought in his commentary on the place.

[42] John 4:2.

Baptism

Another passage of Scripture brought in favour of infant baptism is Acts 2:39: "The promise is to you, and to your children, and to them that are afar off." If the infant children of the Jews have a right to the promise, and therefore to baptism, then on the very same principle all the heathen (for such Peter meant by those who are far off) have a right also, even in their idolatrous state, for the promise is said as much to belong to one as to the other; but the Apostle meant neither the children of the Jews, nor the idolatrous Gentiles, *as such*, for he limits the extent of the promise in the last clause of the verse, even to as many as the Lord our God shall call; and Peter's using this phrase at all, "your children" was probably to remove the fears, which a recollection of their horrid imprecations on themselves and their posterity (when they crucified our Lord) might excite. Then all the people said, "His blood be on us, and our children" (Matt. 27:25). It was a merciful assurance made to their now awakened consciences, that their imprecations, neither on themselves nor on their children, should be any hindrance to their salvation, provided they were effectually called to faith and repentance. Forget not the phrase, even to as many (of you, of your posterity, and of the Gentiles too) as the Lord shall call.

A third passage is in 1 Corinthians 7:14: "The unbelieving husband is sanctified by the wife, and the unbelieving wife is sanctified by the husband, else were your children unclean, but now are they holy." This text stands the foremost in support of the new way of defending infant baptism, which Zuinglius boasts the honour of discovering by 1525 AD, on the grounds of federal holiness.[43] But let it be observed first, the Apostle is not speaking of baptism in the whole connection, and therefore, allowing the holiness here spoken of to mean a relative holiness, it would

---

[43] Huldrich Zwingli, "A Refutation of Baptist Tricks," in *Works*, vol. 3, trans. Preble.

not prove the contested point. Second, after all the contest about relative holiness under the gospel dispensation, nobody can tell what it means; and though it had so much to do with and was highly suited to the Mosaic economy, yet on evangelical principles it can neither be conceived of nor defined. "If any man be in Christ (or a Christian) he is a new creature" (2 Cor. 5:17).

Third, the scope of the chapter shows the Apostle's meaning; the Corinthians thought that as Jews, on their return from Babylon, were commanded to put away their idolatrous wives (Ezra 10:10), so it was incumbent on themselves, being converted to Christianity, to abandon their husbands or wives who still remained in a heathenish state. Paul dissuades them from such a resolution, arguing (v. 16) from the hope of their future conversion; and in the verse under notice, from the stability of the marriage contract notwithstanding the change which had taken place it their normal state. Sanctification means separation to some special use. Now he contends that the mutual choice and voluntary consent of the parties formed a reciprocal separation for the ends of the conjugal relation, and that this legal contract could not be dissolved; for this legitimates the fruits of their union, and so makes them holy: whereas, if their union was not acknowledged to be on these principles, their children would be born of fornication, and so be unclean or illegitimate.

Nor is this interpretation a novel one—it is found among divines of ancient as well as modern date. I will select, for the sake of its brevity, the comment of Ambrose of Milan, who flourished between three and four hundred years after Christ. The "children," says he, "are holy, because born of lawful wedlock."

Baptism

The chief end of baptism answered in believers alone
I proceed thirdly to justify the confining of baptism to professed penitents and believers, because in them alone the chief end of its appointment can be answered.

Various improvements may be made of this institution, but the precise design of our Lord in appointing it appears to be noticed by Paul: "As many of you as have been baptized into Christ, have put on Christ" (Gal. 3:27); that is, by profession. It is a public expression of our embracing the religion of Jesus Christ, and our desire and design of surrendering ourselves entirely to his service. Baptism is the gate of the visible church, not the means of admission into any one distinct society; but the mode of a general profession of repentance towards God, and faith in our Lord Jesus Christ. This the Apostle enumerates with the circumstances of unity among Christians at large (Eph. 4:4–5), where he supposes them to be partakers of the same hope, to be governed by the same Lord, to believe the same truth, and to profess it by one baptism.

The catechism of the established church of this country is to express to this point: "What (it is asked) is required of persons to be baptized?" The answer is repentance, whereby they forsake sin, and faith, whereby they steadfastly believe the promises of God made to them in that sacrament. It is not my business to reconcile such words as these with the application of this ordinance to children. Let every man bear his own burden. But it will be vain to plead the use of sponsors, who promise to repent, believe, renounce the flesh, the world, and the devil, and obey God on the child's behalf. Repentance, faith, and obedience are personal actions, and he that derives his merit from another's faith may with equal propriety draw his comfort from another's salvation. Proxy will hold as good in one case as in the other.

But, if repentance and faith are personal actions to be professed in baptism, how inadequate to the end of baptism must an infant be, who is necessarily incapable of either. Surely, it cannot be hard to prove that as the child of a Christian derives no actual personal qualification from his parent to justify a religious profession, so neither can an involuntary profession, which a newborn babe is compelled to make by its parents, ensure any advantage which an unbaptized child may not equally enjoy. Does baptism wash away sin? Papists may assert this, but Protestants deny it.[44] Is grace given the child in baptism? Has God truly regenerated the child just sprinkled at the font? Is the babe actually made a member of Christ, a child of God, and an inheritor of the kingdom of heaven? Why is it then that persons baptized in infancy are not uniformly pious in their afterlives? How is it so many of them turn out such profligates? Are these the fruits, or the evidences of their regeneration? Are these the persons who may call God their Father, Christ their Head, and heaven their home?

O, when will the day break, and the shadows flee away? When shall Christians surrender their prejudices to reason and revelation; and abandon practices unknown to the Scriptures and tending to the subversion of personal religion?

---

[44] "Peccatorum remissio data est in Christi baptism. Haec tanta est virtus aqua, ut corpus taugat, et cor abluat. Sicut aqua Sordes corporis acvestea abluit; ita baptismus maculas animae sordesque vitiorum emundando abstergit. Haec est res hujus sacramenti, scil. Interior mundicia. Res hujus sacramenti justification est. Omnes in baptism ab peccato mandantur." See Peter Lombard, *Book of Sentences*, ed. 1528. Book 4, Distinctions 3. Pages 48, 40.

That such should be the language of a Catholic Prelate in the twelfth century astonishes nobody; but to see the following sentiments in a modern publication, from a Protestant pen, must amaze the world: "Christ has nothing to do with any man, nor any man with Christ, till he is baptized with water. All power in Heaven and in Earth is in baptism. He that is not baptized has no interest in Father, Son, nor Spirit. By this ordinance he is united unto the true God, and becomes one with him in all things. Baptism is our righteousness and holiness—it is remission and cleansing from sin, and though our sins are red as scarlet, baptism makes white, and whiter than snow. He who is baptized is as white and clean from sin as God can make him." See Thomas Llewellyn's *Treatise on Baptism*. Thomas Llewellyn (c.1720–1783) was a Welsh Baptist.

Baptism

On the solid grounds set before you, we maintain the primitive glory of this institution, as it was maintained by the churches of Christ (for that can be proved to the contrary) for above 200 years; and though the duration or extinction, the popularity or the decline of any sentiment or practice, does not lessen or augment the weight of Scriptural evidence; yet it cannot but be pleasing for us to find that the purest Christian antiquity is on our side.

Baptism through antiquity
Justin Martyr is one of the most eminent uninspired writers of the first ages in the Christian church. He flourished about the middle of the second century. Reports highly injurious to the reputation of the Christians being raised by their enemies, he wrote an apology on their behalf addressed to the emperor Antoninus Pius, in which, after vindicating the Christians from the crimes laid to their charge, he says,

> I will now inform you of the manner, in which on our conversion, we dedicate ourselves to God through Christ, lest if I omitted this, my address might be suspected of insincerity. Whoever are convinced of the truth of our doctrine, and live under its influence, are first directed to pray with fasting, and seek from God the pardon of their sins; we uniting with them in these exercises. Then we bring them to a place of water, and there they are newborn, as we were, for they are washed in the name of God, the Father and Lord of all, and of our Saviour Jesus Christ, and of the Holy Spirit.[45]

Now as Justin professed to give an account of baptism for the very purpose of avoiding any suspicion of disguise, and as he engaged to declare the mode of dedication to God then prac-

---
[45] Justin Martyr, *First Apology*, 61.1-5.

ticed, we might justly infer that there was nothing of importance relative to this ordinance omitted by him; and yet it is plain that he speaks alone of adult, and makes not the least mention of infant baptism. A sufficient proof that the baptism of infants was unknown in the church at the middle of the second century.

Tertullian was one of the chief men among the Christians in the beginning of the third century. He is the very first who speaks expressly of infant baptism, and it is highly worthy of remark, he opposes it as an error, which probably then began to creep into the church.

It is impossible for words to represent ideas so plainly as not to leave them liable in some cases to misinterpretation. This was the case with two sayings of our Saviour, both in John's Gospel: "Unless you eat my flesh and drink my blood, you have no life in you" (John 6:53). This, it was said, meant a participation of the Lord's Supper; and that whosoever did not partake of this ordinance must be damned; hence parents, tenderly concerned for their offspring, and priests for the lambs of their flocks, united in the admission of infants to the Eucharist.[46] The other passage,

---

[46] It is an historical fact, which though but little known, is not unworthy of consideration, that the practice of infant communion was nearly, if not quite as universal as infant baptism is now. It appears to have originated in Africa, where (in the opinion of many) infant baptism was first introduced. Proofs are brought of its existence as early as the time of Cyprian, about the middle of the third century. In the two next centuries, it came more general in the western Church, and prevailed for six hundred years, during which time the custom was adopted by the Eastern Christians, and with them (who form the largest part of Christendom) it continues to this day but the doctrine of the transubstantiation of the elements used in the Lord's Supper, into the real body and blood of Christ, coming into the Romish Church about the year 1000, infant communion fell into disuse, for the same reason that the use of the cup was discontinued to the laity, lest any of the Lord's body and blood should be spilled, and so profaned. Much information on this subject is contained in William Wall, *History of Infant Baptism*, 511.

It appears that infant communion and infant baptism are of the same date, that they both originated in one part of the world, and it is probable that as one is now discontinued by nearly half the Christian church, the other half will be finally annihilated, and both have no existence but in the historical page, to amuse and amaze succeeding generations.

equally misunderstood, was "unless a man be born of water and of the Spirit, he cannot enter into the Kingdom of God" (John 2:5). This being born of water was supposed to mean baptism; and the Kingdom of God, to intend future happiness.[47] It was thence concluded that without baptism their children could never be admitted to the glories of the heavenly world. Where is the wonder that possessed with such ideas, the affectionate parent should earnestly solicit this saving rite on the behalf of his beloved offspring?

Whether any Christian ministers at this time were inclined to favour this practice cannot be ascertained, but it seems as though Tertullian painfully anticipated the progress of the rising error; and the good man thought it his duty to remonstrate. This is his language:

> What need is there of exposing sponsors to danger, since they may be prevented by death from accomplishing their promises, or be disappointed by the evil disposition of their children? Our Lord indeed does say, "Forbid not their coming to me;" but let them come when they are grown up, let them come when they can understand; when they are capable of knowing where they are coming. Let them be made Christians, when they are able to know Jesus Christ. Why should their guiltless age hasten to the remission of sins (or Baptism?). More caution is used in temporal concerns, for you will not commit earthly things to the care of those, whom you entrust with heavenly. Let them be taught to seek after this salvation, that it may appear, you give to him that asks.[48]

---

[47] May not the Kingdom of God here intend the true Church of Christ, or the Gospel dispensation, and so the sense of the ancients on the former part of the verse be admitted: viz. that unless a man was baptized in water and renovated by the Holy Spirit, he could not be a consistent regular member of the visible Church of Christ—the former being essential to a due profession of Christianity, the latter to an interest in its blessings!

[48] Tertullian, *On Baptism*, 18.

It is plain that Tertullian did not understand our Lord's words, "Suffer little children to come to me," as warranting the baptism of infants. On the contrary, he thought them unfit subjects, and therefore he wisely instructs the parents to let them stay till they know Christ, and understand the nature and importance of Christian baptism; and among other things, he declares the inability of infants to make a right use of that solemn ordinance.

But this respectable Father's success was not equal to the goodness of his design. The commonly received notion of baptism washing away sin proved too powerful for all his logic, honesty and eloquence; for, fifty years later, Cyprian (who was the first that vindicated the change of immersion into aspersion) not only approved of baptizing infants himself, but in the name of a council, containing sixty-six bishops or teachers, recommended it to others. It is observable that he grounds the rite not on any command given by our Lord, but on analogical reasoning, and that too of the most puerile kind; for thus he argues that, "if those who had been old offenders were not refused, why should an infant, who had nought but original sin to be forgiven, be denied the grace of Baptism, since such more easily received forgiveness of sin; because they had no sin of their own, but of others to be forgiven them."

The wonder, which this mode of reasoning excites, will subdue when it is known that the writings of this Carthaginian Bishop justify the consecration of the baptismal water—the exorcising of the devil—the necessary use of Chrism, or anointing in baptism, with other superstitious practices which all Protestants now agree to explode. He that pleads for the propriety of infant baptism from such antiquity is not far from the "Holy Catholic Church." But there are two things among others which prove that the practice of infant baptism was not as yet universal.

Baptism

1. Many who afterwards filled distinguished places in the Church, though born of Christian parents, were not baptized till adult; as Gregory, Bishop of Constantinople, Nectarius, his successor, and others.[49]

2. About this time addresses were made to the young people of the congregation to come to baptism.[50] Sermons delivered by Basil, Nazianzen, and others are yet extant, wherein they employ all the powers of rhetoric to induce their youth to receive this sacred rite; but had Christian parents been Paedobaptists in that day, the preacher's eloquence must have been needlessly employed. Mr. Baxter indeed acknowledges that "the words of Tertullian and Nazianzen show, it was long before all were agreed of the very time, or of the necessity of baptizing infants, before any use of reason, in case they were likely to live to maturity."[51]

But the time was now fast approaching when this plant, which had been taking deeper root for above a century, should suddenly expand itself over all the Christian world. Tertullian and Cyprian both lived at Carthage in Africa, the darkest part of Christendom. Augustine also lived in Africa, was bishop of Hippo, and a man of influence and devotion, but he seems to have been deficient in his views of Christian liberty. He espoused the practice which Tertullian had opposed, and was resolved, if possible, to make all professing Christians espouse it too. A council of Bishops met at Carthage (416 AD) to condemn the heresy of Pelagius, and from Carthage fourteen or fifteen of them ad-

---

[49] Robinson, *History of Baptism*, 236.
[50] Robinson, *History of Baptism*, 249.
[51] Richard Baxter, *More Proofs of Infants Church-Membership and Consequently Their Right to Baptism: Or a Second Defence of Our Infant Rights and Mercies* (London, 1675), 279. The words of Nazianzen, to which Mr. Baxter refers, I suppose, are part of a Sermon preached in the year 381, in which he recommends Children's baptism to be administered at the age of three years, except in cases of necessity. How plain are the gradations from a mistaken judgment to an unscriptural practice in the case of infant baptism!

journed to Mela in Numidia. Augustine was president of this council; and under his influence, among other decrees guarded by anathemas, was the following: "It is the pleasure of all the bishops present in the holy Synod to order, that whosoever denies that infants newly born of their mothers are to be baptized, shall be accursed."[52]

This decree was sent to Rome to be ratified, and in consequence all Christians who refused to receive infants into their churches by baptism were anathematized, first by Pope Innocent, then by Pope Zozimus, and afterward by Pope Boniface. At this time, there were four hundred churches in Africa who refused submission to this imperious prelate; their refusal brought on persecution, and it has been said, "it was not Austin's fault, that one was left to tell the barbarous tale."[53] But the Donatists of Africa were not the only Christians whose sufferings for nonconformity to this innovation are on the records of antiquity. Let one instance more suffice—it is more interesting to us because nearer home.

Christianity was planted in this island according to Gildas, our most ancient historian, in the reign of Tiberias Caesar.[54] And though the conquests of the Saxons obliged the British

---

[52] Robinson, *History of Baptism*, 201.

[53] Robinson, *History of Baptism*, 198.

[54] If Gildas be right, Britain must have been favoured with the Gospel within five years after our Lord's crucifixion, for Tiberius died 37 AD. Different accounts are given of the first Christian mission to Britain; some say, Joseph of Arimathea preached at Glastonbury in Somersetshire, and gathered the first church there; others, that the Gospel was planted here by Simon Zealotes; and others, that it was first brought by some Asiatic soldiers. It is certain, however, from Tertullian's well-known observation, that Christianity was introduced here at an early period of the Christian era.

Bishop Newton observes, "There is some probability that the Gospel was preached in Britain by St. Simon the Apostle, there is much greater probability that it was preached here by St. Paul, and there is absolute certainty, 'that Christianity was planted in this country in the days of the Apostles, before the destruction of Jerusalem.'" Thomas Newton, *Dissertations on the Prophecies Which Have Remarkably Been Fulfilled and at This Time Are Fulfilling in the World* (London, 1826), 341.

Christians to flee into Wales, above two thousand dwelt together in a spacious building at Bangor, working with their hands and serving God in peace. But about the year 604, Pope Gregory sent one Augustine of Canterbury, a monk, to convert the Saxons to the Christian faith. Sometime after his arrival he obtained an interview with a deputation from these British Christians, somewhere in Worcestershire, and made every effort to seduce them to the communion of the Roman church. Unsuccessful in his first overtures, he made three proposals as terms of peace: the observation of Easter, giving Christendom to children, and preaching in union with him to the Saxons. The consciences of these men were not flexible enough for the haughty priest, and this professed minister of peace revenged their refusal by setting the Saxons upon them, whereby twelve hundred honest men were martyred, because (among other things) they would not baptize children (or give Christendom to children). It would carry me far beyond the time limited for a public discourse were I to present you with the various instances of Papal (and I blush to add, Protestant) persecution, which in different ages the defenders of believer's baptism have realized.

There is scarcely a country in Europe whose annals will not furnish us with accounts of martyrs in this pious cause, but truth claims deity for its patron, and though long opposed, shall prevail—and there is good reason to expect that this primitive baptism, which I have been defending, will before long be restored to the universal Church of Christ. First, because the ground on which Paedobaptism was originally established, and on which it was for above a thousand years defended, is abandoned by most of the reformed Churches. The plea of purification from original sin has given way to federal holiness, and covenant revelation. Second, the personal nature of the Christian dispensation is better understood than for many ages past. Third, in consequence of this improved understanding, the primitive doctrine of baptism prevails in many places. In this country, there are more favourers of adult baptism than at any period since Augustine got the Saxons to murder the monks at Bangor. In America, where it was once a crime, there were, in 1790 AD, near 900 congregations. These included above 1,100 ordained and licensed ministers and more than 65,000 persons of this profession. Though there had been no remarkable revival in the preceding twelve months, yet 1,500 members had been added to the churches, and 30 new churches constituted[55] and blessed be God. There is one negro church in Africa, and adult Christians, baptized on profession of faith,[56] are the only constituents of this Christian society.

Conclusion

Leaving what has been said to your serious recollection, I conclude with a few remarks.

1. If a divine command or apostolic example be essential to direct Christian worship, then infant baptism is no part of Christian duty, but a mere tradition.

2. If infant baptism be anti-Scriptural, whatever respect we bear to individuals or societies who retain the practice, it becomes the real friends of Christ personally to bear witness against it by publicly dedicating themselves to him in his appointed way.

---

[55] See John Asplund, *The Annual Register of the Baptist Denomination in North America, 1790*, 47. A cheap book full of information on the subject. Since that book was printed, there has been a considerable increase in the state of Virginia. Concerning the prevalence of adult baptism there, a respectable correspondent writes, "In looking over some papers lately, I found in an American letter of 1753, an account is given of the circumstances of the formation of the first Baptist Church in Virginia. It was formed the 8th of October, 1751, with only eleven constituents." Asplund's *Register* informs us, "that in 1790 the Baptist Churches in that State were 204, and the members 20,443—Amazing! Who can tell how many they may be by this time." November 18, 1793.

[56] See John Rippon, *The Baptist Annual Register*, no. 6, 473, where a very interesting account is giving of brother D. George, the Pastor of that Church, from whom I have had recent accounts of its increase prosperity.

3. If a public dedication to Christ be calculated to honour our divine master, the candidates for baptism this morning have a claim on your respect, and their conduct is worthy of your imitation.

4. If baptism be a profession of faith in Christ, and subjection to him, then let us be chiefly concerned for personal religion—without this our profession is vain—nor let us rest here, but remembering that the vows of the Lord are upon us, be careful to walk worthy of our high vocation. Let us be amiable in our tempers, pure in our conversation, and upright in our conduct, ever ready to do good and to communicate. Let us endeavour as much to excel in true morality, as we believe we are more Scriptural in this positive institution.

7
Confession of Faith[1]

1794

Religion of every description originates in the belief of a God, the author of our existence, the preserver of our lives, and the object of our worship.

One God

Convinced from the varied scenes of infinite wisdom, power, and goodness, which present themselves on every hand, I do believe in one self-existent, independent, almighty, omnipotent, and unchangeable Being, who is the great origin of all, who is in all, and through all, and over all, God blessed forevermore. A Being whose majesty teaches me to revere him, his goodness to love him, his faithfulness to trust him, and his universal dominion to worship and adore him.

God's revelation

I believe that this eternal God, for the benefit of his rational creatures in this world, has been pleased to reveal to them, by different modes and in different ages, that information which was necessary for the regulation of their faith and conduct; that what remains of this revelation is contained in the Holy Scriptures, or those books usually called the Old and New Testament; that the books therein contained declare the very mind and will of God, and were written by holy men of old, under his immediate inspi-

---

[1] From Andrew Fuller, *Memoirs of the Rev. Samuel Pearce*, ed. W.H. Pearce (London: G. Wightman, 1831), 8-13. The original is in the Bristol Baptist College Archives, Ms G96 BMS Box 14658. Footnotes indicating Scripture citations and allusions have been kept to a minimum.

ration. I believe that this revelation is so complete as to need no addition, and declares every truth necessary to be believed, and every duty God requires to be performed by man. I believe that its Author has been pleased to give such demonstrations of its authenticity as are wholly adequate to the satisfaction of every honest mind.

By these Scriptures, I am instructed in those important truths which respect the nature, perfections, and operations of God. On their testimony alone, I believe that, though the essence of the Godhead is one, yet there are three who bear record in heaven, the Father, the Word and the Holy Spirit. The Father is truly and properly God; the Son is truly and properly God; and the Holy Spirit truly and properly God; and yet there are not three Gods, but one God, in essence, power, and glory. Though I confess this is a mystery, incomprehensible by mortals, yet on the testimony of Scripture—which I conceive fully and expressly to teach the doctrine of the Trinity in Unity—I submit to the authority of revelation; and, as I cannot fathom, I wish to trust.

Creation

Agreeable to Scripture information, I believe that in the beginning God created the heavens and the earth in six days. Having designed this world for, and suited it to, the condition of a rational creature, he made man in his own image, with a mind formed for loving and obeying its Creator. Yet at the same time, God made man in perfect consistency with that freedom of the will with which, for the honour and justice of divine government, he endues all his intelligent creatures.

The Law

I believe that God wisely appointed a test for the obedience of man, wonderfully suited to his nature and state, promising a continuance of felicity co-equal with a continuance of duty; but threatening death as the consequence of a violation of his law, including not only subjection of the body to mortality, but also a loss of the moral image of God, and liability to everlasting misery, as the just reward of sin.

I believe that man voluntarily and willingly, without any necessity from the purpose of God, did violate this law, and thereby expose himself to all of its penalties. Therefore, from the connection of the whole human race with Adam, all his posterity are so interested in his conduct as through his fate to become possessors of a corrupt nature, which, being opposed to the righteous will of God, constitutes us objects of his displeasure, and disposes us to that conduct which terminates in eternal death. As in the language of Scripture, "Sin having entered into the world, death came by sin, so that death has passed upon all men, for that all have sinned."[2]

Election

I believe that, before the world began, God (foreseeing the dreadful calamities which mankind would bring upon themselves) did, of his own free and sovereign purpose and grace, choose a certain number of the human race to everlasting salvation. He made provision for this display of his mercy, in perfect harmony with the justice of his character, in the covenant of grace, by which all things appertaining to the redemption of the elect were ordered and made sure. I believe that the Son of God, the second person in the adorable Trinity, having thus engaged to effect the salvation of his people, in entire consistency with the divine perfections, did in the fullness of time (agreeably to ancient prophecies) unite himself to human nature, being miraculously conceived by the virgin of the Holy Spirit. In that human nature he obeyed, suffered, and died on behalf of the elect of

---

[2] Romans 5:12.

God, whose sins were imputed to him, and the punishment of which he bore in his own body on the tree, suffering the just for the unjust, to bring them to God, making a plenary satisfaction to almighty justice for all their transgressions, and effecting a complete righteousness, which, being imputed to them on believing, becomes the matter of their justification before God.

The work of Christ

I believe that the sacrifice of Christ is so efficacious, and his righteousness so complete, that for the sake of his merits alone, independently of any holiness of the creature, the transgressions of believers are forgiven, they are reconciled to God, receive the adoption of sons, and become heirs of everlasting glory.

The work of the Holy Spirit

I believe that, for our preparation to eternal life, the work of the Holy Spirit of God in us is as necessary as the work of Christ for us. The Holy Spirit is the author of regeneration, and all its fruits, as repentance, faith, love, hope, joy, peace, purity, and meetness for heaven. All the elect of God have been, are, or shall be made, the subjects of this efficacious grace. None have the least reason to conclude themselves the objects of the divine favour whose hearts are not renewed, and whose lives are not sanctified by this divine Spirit—for "without holiness no man shall see the Lord."[3]

Preservation of the saints

I believe that all those who are thus renewed by the Holy Spirit in the spirit of their minds shall certainly and finally persevere in grace, and attain to everlasting glory, notwithstanding all the opposition they meet with from the world, the flesh, and the

---

[3] Hebrews 12:14.

devil, being "kept by the power of God through faith to salvation."[4]

Intermediate state

I believe that when death puts a period to man's existence, and his body returns to the dust, his soul returns to God who gave it, then to receive an immediate consciousness of its future destiny, in which state it remains, either in certain expectation of unutterable misery, or delightful anticipation of eternal enjoyment, till the judgment day.

Resurrection to judgment

I believe that there will be a resurrection of the dead, both of the just and of the unjust, to which shall succeed the general judgment, when all the human race shall be impartially judged according to the deeds done in the body, whether good or evil. Those who died in a state of impenitency and unbelief shall throughout eternity endure the most exquisite torments, as the due reward of their sins against God. Those who have been interested in the atonement of Jesus Christ, are renewed by grace, and made meet for glory, shall be introduced to everlasting honour and joy, even to God's right hand, "where there is fullness of joy, and pleasures for evermore."[5] At that period, the conduct of the Almighty, however dark and inexplicable to us now, shall be, by all God's intelligent creation, acknowledged just, both in the condemnation of the sinner and the salvation of the saint.

The Church

I believe that in order to accomplish the purposes of the grace of God, respecting the calling, sanctifying, and saving of his people,

---

[4] 1 Peter 1:5.
[5] Psalm 16:11.

Jesus Christ has appointed a Gospel ministry, to continue in the world till the end of time, when all the elect shall be gathered in. It is the duty of all those who are called by grace to unite in Christian communion, and publicly to assemble for the purposes of divine worship. A number of Christians united in one faith, and by mutual consent thus assembling together, yielding obedience to the laws of Jesus Christ, constitute a Christian church.

Baptism

I believe that, in order to become a member of a visible church of Christ, it is necessary that the person be baptized, on a profession of repentance and faith, in the name of the Father, the Son, and the Holy Spirit. That baptism is only scripturally and acceptably administered by the immersion of the body in water. None but believers in the Christian faith have a right to this ordinance.

The Lord's Supper

I believe that, for wise ends, Jesus Christ has appointed the sacrament called the Lord's Supper (or a participation of bread and wine by his people, when assembled together) to be continued in his church, both in remembrance of his vicarious sacrifice for their sins, and also to unite them more to one another in love.

Independence

I believe that a society of Christians, or a Christian church thus formed, is wholly independent of any synod, council, or other ecclesiastical magistracy, and has the sole right of conducting its own affairs (as the choosing of a minister, admission or exclusion of members, and the administration of the various parts of church discipline) without the interference of any man, or body of men whatever, whether civil or ecclesiastical. It is the duty of all the friends of Christianity to withstand every encroachment

Confession of Faith

on the liberties of their conscience, or their conduct, by which the peace and good of society is not injured, that hereby they may prove themselves the true disciples of Him who has said, "my kingdom is not of this world."[6]

Postscript

These are the opinions which, from what I deem sufficient evidence, I profess cordially to embrace. These are the sentiments I have invariably endeavoured to defend since providence led me to this town. These truths I think it my honour to avow before so respectable an assembly this day; and these I mean, through divine assistance, to maintain, defend, and enforce, in my future ministry, unless I should find superior evidence than hitherto I have found in favour of different opinions.

---

[6] John 18:36.

8
Salvation by Free Grace Alone[1]

1795

The Elders and Messengers of the several Baptist Churches, met in Association at Bewdley, Worcestershire, England, May 26-27, 1795. To the Churches they represent:

Dear brethren,

With gratitude to the great Master of assemblies for another pleasing interview with each other, we unite in expressing our most affectionate wishes that you also may be comforted with the same consolations by which we ourselves have been comforted of God.[2] On this side of heaven, indeed, we must not expect our pleasures to be wholly undisturbed. Yet, possessed of that faith which overcomes the world,[3] we should exclaim with the holy apostle, "Thanks be to God, who always causes us to triumph in Christ,"[4] and teaches us, "to glory in tribulations also."[5]

Some causes of grief have been suggested in the various Epistles from the Churches. Among these, in some places, the want of success in bringing souls to Christ; in others, the little zeal and diligence which appear in professors—the death of some, and the unbecoming conduct of others, have been lamented. But, brethren, these are trials from which no age of Christianity, not

---

[1] Circular letter of 1795. Association at Bewdley, Worcestershire, England, May 26th and 27th, 1795.
[2] 2 Corinthians 1:4.
[3] 1 John 5:4.
[4] 2 Corinthians 2:14.
[5] Romans 5:3.

even the apostolic, has been exempted. Let not these things discourage us. He that laid the foundation of his church will build her up. He will not desert the work of his own hands, and though Zion may complain, "The Lord has forsaken me!"[6] it will not be long before he will prove to her joy, that she is "engraven on the palms of his hands, and that her walls are continually before him."[7] It shall yet be said, "Cry out and shout, you inhabitant of Zion, for great is the Holy One of Israel in the midst of you."[8] Amidst our causes of complaint, we are not without some indications of the divine favour. Some of our Churches have enjoyed very comfortable additions, most are in peace, and some, who were last year destitute of pastors, are now agreeably supplied. Nor is it one of the least causes of our joy, that our various congregations still avow their attachment to the Faith once delivered to the Saints.

The point of difference between us and many other professing Christians lies in the doctrine of salvation entirely by grace. Some assert that good works are the cause of justification. Some assert that good works are united with the merits of Christ, and so both contribute to our justification. Others assert that good works neither in whole nor in part justify, but the act of faith. We renounce everything in point of our acceptance with God, excepting his free grace alone which justifies the ungodly[9]—we are still treading in the steps of our venerable forefathers, the compilers of the Baptist Confession of Faith, who thus express themselves, respecting the Doctrine of Justification:

> Those whom God effectually calls, he also freely justifies, for Christ's sake alone; not by imputing faith itself, the act

---

[6] Isaiah 49:14.
[7] Isaiah 49:16.
[8] Isaiah 12:6.
[9] Romans 4:5.

Salvation by Free Grace Alone

of believing, or any other evangelical obedience, to them as their righteousness; but by imputing Christ's obedience to the whole law, and passive obedience in his death for their whole and sole righteousness, they receiving and resting on him and his righteousness by faith [which is] the alone instrument of justification.[10]

In this point do all the other lines of our confession meet. If it be admitted that justification is an act of free grace in God, without any respect to the merit or demerit of the person justified, then the doctrines of Jehovah's sovereign love in choosing to himself a people from before the foundation of the world—his sending his Son to expiate their guilt—his effectual operations upon their hearts, and his perfecting the work he has begun in them, until those whom he justifies he also glorifies,[11] will be embraced as necessary parts of the glorious scheme of our salvation.

At this doctrine, therefore, has the chief force of opposition been directed, and various are the modes in which it has been attacked. Sometimes it has been attacked by appeals to our passions, then to our reason, and at other times to the Scriptures. We hope, brethren, you are too well read in your Bibles to be at a loss for weapons of defence against these assaults, since whatever the passions or opinions of men may plead, those holy oracles assure us that we are justified freely by the grace of God, and that he has mercy on whom he will.[12] But there is another mode of attack as frequently and vigorously pursued as either of the former. It is asserted that our doctrine "involves in it conclusions inconsistent with religion, both natural and revealed—that it gives an unjust and offensive idea of God—that it relaxes the

---

[10] *The Second London Confession of Faith* 11.1-2 in William L. Lumpkin, *Baptist Confessions of Faith* (Rev. ed.; Valley Forge, PA: Judson Press, 1969), 265-266.
[11] Romans 8:30.
[12] Romans 3:24; 9:15-16.

obligations of men to faith and holiness—that it withholds consolation from penitent sinners, and saps the foundations of true morality in the world." These are serious charges, and if they can be substantiated, we shall do well to exchange our creed for a better one. But let us examine with what propriety such consequences are charged on our profession.

A doctrine of arbitrary rejection

Because we maintain the free salvation of God's elect, we are accused of holding the doctrine of the "absolute reprobation of all the rest of mankind, so as to involve in it this horrible consequence, that God creates innumerable souls to be inevitably damned without the least compassion for them."

That to choose some, implies to leave others, must be granted; and if nothing more were meant by the charge of free election involving in it the doctrine of reprobation, we should not object to the statement. However, is there no difference between leaving men to the just fruit of their sins, and creating them for inevitable damnation irrespective of their characters? We cheerfully avow our abhorrence of a doctrine which asserts that an infinitely good God created a number of immortal beings capable of such strong sensations of misery as man merely to gratify himself in filling them with the fullness of torment forever. Such a sanguinary Deity we could never love, nor would faith in such a being promote that disposition to gentleness, tenderness, and affection for all mankind, which are everywhere represented in the gospel as the genuine fruits of a spiritual acquaintance with the true character of God. On the contrary, such views of the Almighty would rather cherish the spirit of a bloody Mahomet than a bleeding Jesus.

But we conceive that our detestation of such a creed is in no way inconsistent with our cordial assent to the doctrine of the sovereignty of divine mercy. In much the same way as the execution of a malefactor is not to be attributed to the cruelty of a prince, because royal clemency is a displayed towards another transgressor, so neither do the sovereign acts of God's mercy, in any respect, necessitate him to be the author of misery, any farther than as the author of that holy law which men have broken, and the maintaining of its rights.

In saving, he acts like a merciful Sovereign; in condemning, as a righteous Judge, bound to support the honour of his moral government. He was no more under obligation to save all, than he was to save any; and if salvation itself be an act of grace, surely the author of salvation is at full liberty without any impeachment of his goodness, to display that grace "according to the pleasure of his own will."[13] Is it not admitted, that "all have sinned, and come short of the glory of God?"[14] Is it any act of injustice in Jehovah to punish sin? Would he not have been just in condemning all, because "all have sinned?" How, then, can God's decree make that arbitrary, which, without such a decree, is not more than just? If actual condemnation of the sinner be righteous, the purpose of God to execute his righteous severity towards impenitent sinners cannot be lawfully arraigned.

In these most decided terms, therefore, we disavow the charge of holding a doctrine which, by necessary consequence, involves an arbitrary reprobation of any man, irrespective of his crimes. We are most fully persuaded that nothing can be more ungrateful or more unjust than to represent that as a cause of misery which is the only source of all the mercy ever showed to man, or comfort enjoyed by him in this world or in the next.

---

[13] Ephesians 1:11.
[14] Romans 3:23.

A doctrine which diminishes God's grace

The doctrine of sovereign distinguishing grace is represented as injurious to "the rich goodness, great mercy, and compassion of God to the sons of men; and the contrary doctrine," it is said, "tends more highly to the promotion of God's glory; because, the more there are benefited, the greater is the glory of the benefactor."

But, brethren, let it be considered, that no other doctrine, save that of distinguishing grace, secures the eternal benefit of a single individual of our race; for such is the deep depravity of the human heart, that all the outward means of grace are of themselves totally ineffectual to man's everlasting salvation; insomuch, that after Christ himself had employed the best of external means with the Jews, he complains: "You will not come to me that you might have life;"[15] and upon this ground he asserts, "No man can come to me, except the Father who has sent me draw him."[16] Whence it follows that had not God sovereignly chosen some, and resolved on their salvation, then the death of Christ, and the ministration of the gospel with all its appendages would have been in vain. See, therefore, that the sovereign purpose and effectual operations of Jehovah, so far from diminishing his grace tend highly to exalt it, since it is abundantly evident that there is more "grace, goodness, and compassion," manifested in securing the salvation of some than in making ineffectual provision for the salvation of all.

A doctrine which diminishes the obligation to believe

If the doctrine of distinguishing grace be true, we are told, "then the Jews could not be reasonably accused for not coming to Christ or not believing in him; much less could it be imputed to

---

[15] John 5:40.
[16] John 6:44.

Salvation by Free Grace Alone

them as their great crime, that they would not come to him or believe in him."

Now, that our Lord did accuse the Jews for not coming to him and believing in him, and that justly, we do not deny, but is there anything in the doctrine of salvation by grace which lessens the authority of the gospel, or the obligations of men to embrace it? What more does the gospel require of men than to believe what is true, to love what is good, to do what is right, and to be sorry for what is wrong? And is it possible for any acts of divine mercy to make these obligations cease? If Christianity be properly attested, ought it not to be believed? If God is good, ought he not to be loved? If the commandments of Christ are right, should they not be obeyed? And if he discovers to us our faults, ought we not to repent of them? All these in fact are natural duties arising from our necessary relation to the great God as our creator and moral governor, and it can never be demonstrated that God's special designs of grace to some, annihilate the obligations of all the rest, any more than an earthly prince's discovering extraordinary regard to some of his subjects, releases all his other subjects from their allegiance to him, and subjection to the laws.

The obligations of men to believe the gospel arise from its being a divine revelation worthy of God and sufficiently attested. The obligations to obey the divine precepts are founded on their equity and their being enjoined by the authority of the moral governor of the world, so that unless it can be proved that God has no legal claim to the respect and obedience of any besides those whom he resolves to save, and whose hearts he effectually inclines to keep his law, this objection has no force. If it be admitted, it leaves every man who is not eventually saved at full liberty, without blame, to treat the blessed God of truth as a liar and tyrant! Our doctrine by no means diminishes the guilt of man in rejecting the gospel, but allows us most cordially to unite with a celebrated writer of our own denomination, Dr. John Gill, in asserting that:

> a man not coming to Christ, when revealed in the external ministry of the gospel, as God's way of salvation, is criminal and blameworthy, since the disability and perverseness of his will are not owing to any decree in God, but to the corruption and vitiosity of his nature through sin; and, therefore, since his vitiosity of nature is blameworthy (for God made man upright), that which follows upon it, and is the effect of it, must be so too.[17]

A doctrine which diminishes good works

The doctrine of the sovereignty of divine mercy is charged with being "unfriendly to Christian activity, weakening the motives to diligence in religion, and thereby promoting the disuse of the means of grace."

We hope, brethren, that none of you, by your conduct, have put this objection into the mouths of your adversaries. If you have, the reproach is upon you, not on the truth you profess. Do we not acknowledge the means as much a part of the divine plan as the end? And will not the same objections lie against the providential government of God as are urged against the doctrine of sovereign salvation?

Let us inquire—do you believe in a providence? Is that providence universal? And does it not secure the accomplishment of its immense designs? All this you allow, yet does your confidence in a providence annihilate your industry? Are you husbandmen, and do you expect to reap where you have not sown? Are you merchants, and do you expect to raise an edifice without labor? Is not the time of your life appointed, but do you, on this account, neglect the use of medicine in sickness, and food when in

---

[17] John Gill, *The Course of God and Truth* (London: Aaron Ward, 1735), 1:159-160.

Salvation by Free Grace Alone

health? You attend to these as means necessary to the end. No less necessary do we consider the use of religious means in order to salvation; and from the very same motives, and on the self-same principles on which you act in relation to the concerns of this life, do we conduct ourselves under the influence of our faith in the plans of grace, knowing that "what a man sows that shall he also reap;"[18] and, "for all these things God will be sought to by the house of Israel, to do it for them."

A doctrine which diminishes holiness

The doctrine of distinguishing grace is charged with "giving encouragement to careless sinners to presume groundlessly on God's favour; and discouraging those who are willing to forsake sin from so doing, or cause them to despair of mercy." But how can that doctrine encourage the careless sinner, which in terms the most decided declares the destruction of sin to be the ultimate object of God's designs? Is not the salvation to which we are chosen, represented by us as "through sanctification of the Spirit"? And are not God's elect predestined to conformity to the character of the Son of God, who was holy, harmless, undefiled? And surely, to believe firmly that it is the design of God, that his people "should be holy and without blame before him in love,"[19] can have no tendency to "encourage careless sinners to presume on his favour."

That some hypocrites have abused the doctrine of grace, we admit; but what good thing exists which has not been abused by wicked men? Thousands, from the forbearance of God, take encouragement fully to set their hearts in them to do evil.[20] But does their sin diminish the divine compassion? Do gluttony and drunkenness prove food to be poison? Or tyranny and despotism

---

[18] Galatians 6:7.
[19] Ephesians 1:4.
[20] Ecclesiastes 8:2.

disprove the necessity or excellence of good government? Because there are some who turn the grace of God into lasciviousness, must the crime be imputed to the profession? Or shall those who are friendly to the doctrine of grace be charged with sinning that grace may abound? God forbid![21]

And what is there in this doctrine discouraging to a true penitent? Men that are careless about their salvation cannot be called penitents, nor can they be discouraged from pursuing an object which they have no sincere desire to obtain. As to those who are seeking the kingdom of God and his righteousness with their whole heart and with their whole soul, they are actually in possession of the fruits and evidences of God's distinguishing grace. Can it discourage them to know that their holy desires and spiritual activity are beginnings of a saving work of God upon their hearts, and that he always perfects what he begins? Is this discouraging? No, brethren, you and thousands more have derived encouragement and comfort from such views as these which have "filled you with joy and peace in believing,"[22] and put a new song into your mouths, even praise to the God of your salvation.

A doctrine which diminishes salvation by works

It is urged that the doctrine of distinguishing grace is "injurious to personal religion, as it destroys all hope of obtaining salvation by our own performances."

To this we reply, firstly, this doctrine does not constitute our performances worse in themselves, or less beneficial in their effects, but only takes for granted a certain truth, namely, our own righteousness is insufficient for our salvation. Therefore, unless

---

[21] Romans 6:1–2.
[22] Romans 5:13.

it be injurious for a man to know the truth of himself respecting the depravity of his heart, this doctrine can never injure him.

Secondly, if personal religion can be no other ways promoted than by consideration of its meritorious influence, then we allow that our doctrine destroys it. Yes, so far are we from imagining that real religion, such as the law requires and God approves, can be advanced by the hope of a deserved recompense, that we judge nothing can more effectually subvert it.

Real religion consists in supreme love to God and disinterested love to man. This is "not only the source and principle, but the very sum and substance, nay the perfection of holiness," but service long and painful may be yielded for the hope of reward without any affection to the work, or esteem for the employer, and therefore, without any real religion.

The tendency of any doctrine to promote personal piety is the same as its tendency to promote supreme love to God. As all esteem rises from some real or supposed excellency in its object, whatever exhibits the great Jehovah in the true loveliness of his character, must undoubtedly be calculated to improve our love for him. Now let it be considered with candor whether the doctrine we maintain does not so represent the great Jehovah, as most effectually to engage the admiration and esteem of every holy being in the universe.

The doctrine of distinguishing grace, when simplified, is summed up in three propositions:

1. All men have rebelled against God, and so rendered themselves obnoxious to his everlasting wrath.

2. It is the pleasure of God, for the sake of Jesus Christ, to extend a gracious pardon to a great number of his rebellious creatures, and receive them into his favour as though they had never sinned.

3. God does not extend his purpose of salvation to all, but while he saves some, leaves others exposed to the awful conse-

quences of their crimes, and the righteous awards of his most holy law.

This is a fair statement of the doctrine. Let Jehovah then be viewed in his true character, "The judge of the whole earth,"[23] and what measures could the supreme Governor have pursued more becoming his name as the God of mercy, and his character as the universal judge?

Justice, though an awful characteristic, is nevertheless an essential part of the judicial system; therefore, it is yet beautiful and lovely. Could we feel any esteem for the official character of a human minister of justice, who made a point of pardoning every criminal, let his crimes be as complicated or aggravated as they might? What licentiousness would he thereby introduce! What an encourager would he be of vice, and what an enemy to society! Of what advantage would be his tribunal, and of what avail his office? Here we are persuaded that justice is essential to the loveliness of a legislator's character. Under whatever regulations his designs of mercy may be in his own breast, it is by threatening sin in general with punishment, and by actually punishing a great number of transgressors, that he best maintains the respectability of his office, and preserves order in that society of whose morals he is the guardian. Men will be most effectually deterred from evil by their knowing him to be a determined enemy to vice, and seeing that none have any security but in their innocence. Whereas, if justice were never administered, every man would do what was right in his own eyes, and the world would be filled with blasphemy, rebellion, and every evil work.

Yet as the legislator acts for the good of society, wherever he perceives that clemency may be shown without endangering the public good, it will be an addition to his loveliness to display it—especially if after a series of experiments, it appears to the

---

[23] Psalm 94:2.

Salvation by Free Grace Alone

whole community that such acts of grace under the regulations of legislative wisdom have been to their advantage. Then they will cheerfully leave the exercise of mercy to the discretion of their judge, and from experience be persuaded that it will never be manifested to their injury, they will feel satisfaction and pleasure in every renewed instance of grace; and the disposition which the legislator shows to the exercise of clemency, whenever it is consistent with the honor of his government and the good of the community, will perfect their sentiments of his official beauty and loveliness.

Such, then, is the legislative beauty of Jehovah, that he vindicates the honor of his government, by permitting the law to take its course, and thus shines in the glory of holiness. Yet in this office he is mingling mercy with equity, and forgiveness with justice, according to the counsel of his own will.[24] Every holy mind on a survey of his judicial character must exclaim, "He is the chief of ten thousand; he is altogether lovely." Hence, the doctrines we avow, when rightly understood, are calculated to create and cherish, that mixture of veneration and delight, in our contemplation of the blessed, wherein the essence of divine love and all true religion consist.

To this objection it may be answered, thirdly. Personal religion can never be injured by a right view of God's design in his gracious discriminations; because personal religion was the very thing for which he set apart his people, even "that they should be a peculiar people, zealous of good works."[25] Taught then by our Bibles, that God chose us that we should be holy, we can no longer consider ourselves as possessed of the evidences of election, than while we enjoy in a measure the end of it. Hence we have a motive continually arising from the doctrine itself, to

---

[24] Ephesians 1:11.
[25] Titus 2:14.

"give all diligence to make our calling and election sure,"[26] being convinced, that neither our believing the doctrine, nor expecting to be saved by it are proofs of our security, any further than attended with inward and personal religion.

Concluding exhortation

Thus brethren, we have endeavored to assist you in maintaining "the faith once delivered to the saints."[27] We have only a few exhortations to annex in relation to this subject.

Do not seek controversy

While we wish you to be furnished with weapons of defence in case of an attack, we exhort you not to seek occasions of controversy with your fellow Christians. The religion of the heart generally declines as a controversial disposition prevails. It greatly injures the spirituality of the mind, and its effects everywhere demonstrate that those who indulge it are leaving the wheat for the chaff. To have Christians all of one mind is certainly, in some respects highly desirable, but we must unite with the great Dr. Owen in expecting that, should so delightful a period be ever known on this side heaven, the unanimity of Christians in sentiment will be the fruit of a previous spirit of love. Therefore, with affectionate ardor, we would urge upon you the excellent exhortations which were given by our venerable predecessors, the pastors of more than one hundred Baptist churches above a century ago. Having expressed their anxiety that while they defended the truth, they might carry themselves modestly and humbly towards those who differed from them. They add,

> And, O that, other contentions being laid asleep, the only care and contention of all upon whom the name of the

---

[26] 2 Peter 1:10.
[27] Jude 1:3.

blessed Redeemer is called, might for the future be to walk humbly with our God, and in the exercise of all love and meekness towards each other, to perfect holiness in the fear of the Lord, each one endeavoring to have his conversation such as becomes the gospel, and also suitable to his place and capacity, vigorously promoting in others the practice of true religion and undefiled in the sight of God our Father; and that in this backsliding day, we might not spend our breath in fruitless complaints of the evils of others, but may everyone begin at home to reform in the first place our own hearts and ways, and then to quicken all that we may have influence upon to the same work; that if the will of God were so, none might deceive themselves by resting in, and trusting to, a form of godliness, without the power of it, and inward experience of the efficacy of those truths that are professed by them.[28]

Meekness and prudence in controversy
If you are called upon to defend the truth, see that it be done with meekness and prudence. If the former be wanting you will disgrace yourself—if the latter, the cause you espouse. "The professed friends of truth," says the eminent Dr. Witherspoon,

> often injure the truth; they speak in such a manner as to confirm and harden enemies in their opposition to it. They use such incautious expressions as do indeed justify the objection, "Shall we sin that grace may abound?" And in the heat of their zeal against the self-righteous legalist, seem to state themselves as enemies in every respect to the Law of God, which is "holy, just, and good."[29]

---

[28] *The Baptist Confession of Faith* (1688), Introduction.
[29] John Witherspoon, *Essay on the Connexion Between the Doctrine of Justification by the Imputed Righteousness of Christ and Holiness of Life* (2nd ed.; Edinburgh, 1756), 11-12 (Adapted by Pearce).

Remember, brethren, that it is impossible for God to injure his own government, and set aside his own authority over his creatures; therefore, such modes of defending the truth as have any tendency to diminish the claims of Jehovah, or the obligations of men, must be unwarranted and indefensible.

Shine as lights on earth
Pray that your spirituality of mind, heavenly conversation, and holiness of conduct, may demonstrate to a gainsaying world, that the grace of God, which brings salvation, teaches you habitually and decidedly to deny ungodliness and evil works, and to live soberly, and righteously, and godly in the present evil world. So shall you shine as lights on the earth, and by your good words will glory redound to you Father who is in heaven. To his paternal arms and heart, we now commend you, resting in the fellowship of the gospel.

Your affectionate brethren in the Lord.

9
Ordination Sermon for W. Belsher[1]

Dec 7, 1796

"He gave some—pastors and teachers."
Ephesians 4:11

My Christian Brethren,

Although I partake of your pleasure in this public recognition of the interesting relation which you have formed with our dear brother, yet, I could have wished that the duties which now devolve on you were to be stated and enforced by some more experienced minister. Of one whose better knowledge would have furnished you with more suitable instruction, and whose superior years would have attached a greater weight to his advice. However, since you have requested me to undertake this part of the solemn service of the day, I will endeavor, with affectionate fidelity, to discharge it, hoping that the Head of the Church may put some treasure into the earthen vessel, and enrich and comfort us all with his presence.

The words of my text with the preceding verses are designed to illustrate, to connect, and to confirm some predictions in the Old Testament.

In the sixty-eighth psalm, the prophet having in view some illustrious conqueror, thus celebrates his triumphs: "You have

---

[1] Samuel Pearce, *The Duty of Churches to Regard Ministers as the Gift of Christ* in John Ryland and his, *The Duty of Ministers to be Nursing Fathers to the Church; and the Duty of Churches to Regard Ministers as the Gift of Christ* (London: Button/Worcester: Baskerfield/Birmingham: Belcher/Bristol: James, 1796), 40-62.

ascended on high, you have led captivity captive, you have received gifts for men."[2] This prophecy the apostle illustrates, by teaching that the triumphant language of the psalmist designates the ascension of Jesus Christ, when "having spoiled principalities and powers, he made a show of them openly, triumphing over them by his cross, and took his seat at the right hand of God."[3]

In the third chapter of Jeremiah's prophecy, the Lord comforted his people by promising to "give them pastors according to his heart, who should feed them with knowledge and understanding."[4] Now Paul connects prophesy by declaring that the gifts which the psalmist says the Messiah received for men were the same as the pastors and teachers, which, by Jeremiah, were promised to the church; and he confirms the joint prediction by appealing to manifest and multiplied proofs of its accomplishment, in the persons of "apostles, prophets, evangelists, pastors and teachers,"[5] which, at that very time, were employed for the edification of the disciples of Christ.

Apostles and prophets, in the strict sense of the terms, are no longer upon the earth, because the peculiar and miraculous powers with which they were invested are no longer necessary in the church. Yet, such gifts as are adapted to the church's circumstances are not withheld. You, my brethren, are put in possession of one today—a pastor, to feed you with knowledge and understanding. You have requested me to introduce, as it were, your minister among you. How can I better fulfill your desire, than by presenting him to you as the gift of Christ, and earnestly recommending you, as such, to receive him now, and, as such, invariably to consider him in future.

---

[2] Psalm 68:18.
[3] Colossians 2:14–15.
[4] Jeremiah 3:15.
[5] Ephesians 4:11.

Ministers of Christ, my brethren, like most other blessings, are overvalued by some and held in too little esteem by others. Happy will it be, if you are enabled to find out and preserve the medium between those extremes; and happy shall I account myself, if I am enabled to assist you in regulating your regards for the servant of God, whom you have freely chosen for you pastor.

The passage I have selected, places your minister exactly in that point of view in which you cannot behold him without respect, at the same time that it secures you from esteeming the servant above his Lord. It teaches you to regard him as a gift, but, at the same time, a gift not to be despised. For, he is the gift of Christ. "To every one of us," says the apostle in the preceding verses, "is given grace according to the measure of the gift of Christ—he gave gifts to men," and among other of his gracious bestowments, "he gave some—pastors and teachers."[6]

From various remarks, which are suggested by the consideration of ministers being the gifts of Christ, let us select a few that may be suitable to the present occasion.

The blessed redeemer exercises care over his church on earth

When our Lord gave his last instructions to his apostles, he encouraged them and their successors to obedience by promising to be with them always, even to the end of time.[7] He soon began to fulfil this promise, when on the day of Pentecost he so remarkably "endued them with power from on high,"[8] and attended their ministry with such wonderful efficacy, that the very persons who were hardened under the groans of the Master, now melt under the words of his servants, and joyfully become the disciples of him whom they had crucified.

---

[6] Ephesians 4:7, 11.
[7] Matthew 28:20.
[8] Luke 24:49.

Powerful opposition from the world followed the prosperity of the church:

> The Kings of the earth and the rulers took counsel together against the Lord and against his anointed; but he that sits in the heavens laughed them to scorn; the Lord had them in derision—he spoke to them in his wrath, in his sore displeasure he vexed them.

And triumphing over their subtilty and power, he says, "Yet have I set my king upon my holy hill of Zion."[9]

Persecuted and despised as it was, yet "the truth ran and was glorified." Neither the influence of princes, the terror of armies, the pride of learning, the ignorance of the barbarian, the prejudices of the Jew, nor the threatening nor the tormenting of scourges, racks, or fires, could prevent its prevalence; and though the instruments employed in its propagation were, for the most part, destitute of the ornaments of science or the support of civil power, yet, "mightily grew the word of the Lord, and prevailed."[10]

Many indeed of the faithful ministers of Jesus suffered in his service, and sealed the truth they had propagated with their blood. The church was bereaved of those precious gifts of Christ, while some of its members were martyred with their pastors, and others lived to bewail their loss. Yet while the enemy was thus impoverishing the city of God, Jesus was "leading captivity captive," and, with the spoils he took from the foe, he still enriched and adorned Jerusalem. Those who were "breathing out threatenings and slaughter"[11] against the men who called on the Savior's name, were subdued by the power of his grace and became

---

[9] Psalm 2:2, 4–6.
[10] Acts 19:20.
[11] Acts 9:1.

Ordination for W. Belsher

"preacher of the faith they had once destroyed."[12] If the Jews stone Stephen, the deacon, the church shall have Paul, the apostle, in his room. If the hearers of the gospel be driven from Jerusalem, they shall "preach it at Phenice, and Cyprus, and Antioch."[13]

The more persecution prevailed, the more it called forth the powers and the graces of the faithful. The weak became strong; the timid became bold; the indolent became active; zeal warmed the heart and inspired the tongue. Fresh pastors and teachers were still raised up, and their labors were attended with great success, for "the Lord added daily to the church such as should be saved."[14]

The same process has more or less been carrying on ever since. Whether the pastors of Christ's flock have been removed by means of violence, or by a natural death, their places have again been occupied; and in many instances by those who have excelled their predecessors in piety, wisdom, and success.

When the Hebrew Christians mourned over their deceased teachers, how did the apostle comfort their hearts, but by reminding them that "Jesus Christ is the same yesterday, today, and forever!"[15] The history of nearly eighteen centuries gives stability to this ground of consolation. Behold a new evidence of it today! Behold another proof that our Lord remembers his church, "now he is in his kingdom!" and may the recollection of this day enliven your hope, my brethren, and establish your confidence should you live to attend your present pastor to the tomb! Though Christ has presented you with a valuable gift, you must not forget that it is a mortal one—a vessel, which, though it

---

[12] Galatians 1:23.
[13] Acts 11:19.
[14] Acts 2:47.
[15] Hebrews 13:8.

contains a heavenly treasure, is composed of earthly materials, and may soon be broken.

We should never form an earthly connection without reflecting on the certainty of its dissolution—the husband and his wife, the parent and the child, dear and soft as those relations are, must think of parting; and you, my brethren, must part with your minister. Should such an event be occasioned by any improper behavior on your part, the Lord may correct you for your sin by withholding a blessing you abuse, but should your pastor be taken away by the hand of God, comfort yourselves with the thought that ministers are the gifts of Christ, that he can easily replace your loss, and that his continued care over his church, lays a ground of expectation that it will be so.

Obligations under a faithful pastor bring a peculiar gratitude

Every good thing we enjoy comes from above,[16] and therefore demands our thankfulness; but singular blessings demand singular acknowledgments—to those who know how to value it aright, there are a few gifts to be more highly prized than a worthy minister. The difficulty which you, my brethren, have found in replacing your late pastor must have convinced you that a suitable successor is no common favour. A man of piety, prudence, zeal, and other ministerial gifts is a scarce commodity which no human labor can produce, nor wealth procure. If obtained, he can be only enjoyed as the gift of Christ.

Above five years you have been seeking, and, I presume, praying for a spiritual guide. Your prayers are now answered. Many churches in the same situation have been waiting and praying for a similar blessing. Our brother might have been given to them instead of you. Consider yourselves as peculiarly favoured and be peculiarly grateful.

---

[16] James 1:17.

They ought to be highly esteemed for Christ's sake

True friendship prizes a gift more for the giver's sake than for its intrinsic value. Though I would not suggest that ministers have a less claim on the affections and respect of a people than other good men, yet it is as the gifts of Christ that they demand peculiar regard. As long as they conduct themselves in a manner worthy the exalted office they sustain, so long their Master says to them, "he that receives you, receives me."[17] And the becoming or unbecoming conduct of their people to them, Christ considers as to himself, and he will say respecting both the one and the other at last, "Inasmuch as you did it to one of the least of these my brethren, you did it to me."[18]

Possessed with this idea of your minister, you will be always disposed to view his person and his ministry in the most favourable light; and should you perceive an imperfection in your pastor (for to absolute perfection what modern pastor can pretend, when an apostle disclaimed it?)[19] You will either bury it in his virtues, or cover it with the mantle of your own affections.

As the gift of Christ to you, your minister stands in a relation interesting and intimate—he is become, as it were, your property; but this, so far from allowing you to treat him with severity or neglect, is designed to endear him to you the more. For no man is supposed to "hate his own flesh, but on the contrary nourish it and cherish it, even as the Lord the church."[20] Indeed, when a man devotes his time with his bodily and mental powers for a people's good, equity to him, requires the return of affection and respect; but how much more compulsory is the demand when his person, his graces, and his ministerial endowments are considered as the gift of Christ!

---

[17] John 13:20.
[18] Matthew 25:40.
[19] Philippians 3:12.
[20] Ephesians 5:29.

They should be improved for the purposes bestowed

This is the last observation I shall make on the sentiment of the text, and to this I wish more amply to engage your attention.

None of God's gifts are bestowed without design—the falling shower and the clear shining of the sun after rain, the wintry frosts and the summer heats, have their respective uses; nor can you suppose that the great Head of the Church has called our brother by his grace, put him into the ministry, and given him to you as a pastor, without having in view some important end. It will now be your wisdom, as it is your duty, to consider seriously what that end is, and to be practically concerned to have it answered.

Plainly is this design unfolded in the words following the text, "for the perfecting of the saints, for the work of the ministry, for the edifying of the body of Christ."[21] That is not for your increase in numbers only, but also for your improvement in wisdom and goodness. Now your duties, my brethren, are consequent on your pastors. If he be a teacher, you must be learners. If he has a building to erect, you must be fellow laborers; and unless you be wanting in the duties of your stations, you may be assured that the divine blessing will not be withheld.

You must be much in prayer for your minister

His work is great, and the necessary qualifications for the discharge of it are neither unimportant nor few. It requires much wisdom to understand the Scriptures. It requires much fortitude to oppose the errors, the indifference, and the impurities of the times. It requires much zeal to labor extensively and habitually for Christ and souls, much prudence to advise and act in difficult cases, and much personal religion to impart a savor of Christ to all his conversation, his discourse, and his prayers.

---

[21] Ephesians 4:12.

Ordination for W. Belsher

Here then is scope for your petitions: the furniture of a Christian minister must come from above, and from there it must be sought. "Brethren, pray for us,"[22] said the apostle of the Gentiles—brethren, pray for us, we also say. Men of like passions with yourselves—exposed to temptation from numerous quarters, as prone naturally to depart from God as you, liable to stupidity, carnality, and vanity—then pray for us. O, if you have any desire to see us holy, spiritual, active, honorable, then pray for us.

You are not unacquainted, brethren, with the difficulties which lie in the way of our success. The labor of the Carthaginian general is not to be compared with ours![23] What are the stony Alps to a stony heart, or what the Roman legions to the powers of darkness—"to spiritual wickedness in high places!" Not merely to inform the judgments, to excite the passions, to conquer the prejudices of education, and to reform the manners of men, are before us—a more arduous task presents itself. My brethren, our point is not gained without a change of heart. A renovation of the whole soul. A conversion from the power of Satan to God. But who is sufficient for these things?[24] Can human energy affect them? Nay, my brethren, we are compelled to own that "we are not sufficient of ourselves to do anything as of ourselves—all our sufficiency is of God."[25] Were all the moral virtues, and supernatural endowments which have ever adorned the saint, or distinguished the apostle, concentrated in one Christian pastor, neither will believers be improved; nor sinners converted without the presence, the power, and the grace of Christ! In vain we enter the pulpit; in vain we persuade, we ex-

---

[22] 1 Thessalonians 5:25.
[23] A reference to Hannibal's infamous journey through the alps to attack Rome during the Second Punic War, 218 BC.
[24] 2 Corinthians 2:16.
[25] 2 Corinthians 3:5.

hort, we beseech, we reprove, we warn, or we invite. The Word will never come with a saving power unless it "come in the Holy Spirit."

A faithful address to a guilty conscience may make a Roman governor tremble. "The manifestation of the truth," may "almost persuade a Jewish monarch to become a Christian." But to bring a sinner from "darkness to light—to translate him from the kingdom of Satan, into the kingdom of God's dear Son,"[26] to constitute those who were "aliens from Israel without hope and without God in the world, fellow citizens with the saints and of the household of God,"[27] is a work which would be presumption for an archangel to undertake, and can only be accomplished by him with whom "nothing is impossible."[28] Our only encouragement to labor, and our only hope of success, arises from the promise of God, and as a means of enjoying it, the prayers of our people. My dear brethren, you had better dispose of your pastor to some other church, unless you have a heart to pray for him.

Make your minister's work as easy as you can

I do not mean by abridging the duties of his office but by rendering him as easy, both in preparing for them and engaging in them as you are able. In proportion as his heart is in the work of God, so may that work be expected to prosper in his hand. It must be your care to prevent or remove, as much as possible, whatever might divert his mind from the immediate concerns of the relation in which he now stands to you. As the apostle advises Timothy, he may "give himself wholly to them," or literally "be in them."[29] For this purpose, two things especially demand your concern.

---

[26] Colossians 1:14.
[27] Ephesians 2:12, 19.
[28] Luke 1:37.
[29] 1 Timothy 4:15.

He is provided for
First, that such provision be made for his support as may free his mind from all anxieties respecting his domestic affairs. For a minister to owe a bill which he cannot discharge, or to want a meal which he cannot obtain, is enough to turn his dwelling into a prison, and will sooner or later weaken his mind too much for studious application at home, or vigorous efforts abroad.

The duty of ministerial support is enforced in the Scriptures with energetic plainness. "Do you not know," says the apostle, "that those who minister about holy things live of the things of the temple? And they who wait at the altar are partakers of the altar? Even so has the Lord ordained that they who preach the gospel should live of the gospel," and in verse 11, "if we have sown to you spiritual things, is it a great thing if we shall reap your carnal things?"[30]

Such language as this convinces our judgments while it binds our conscience. It is the language not merely of authority, but of justice. While it forbids our disobedience, it compels us to acknowledge that to obey is our reasonable service; especially when we consider that had the man who consecrates himself to the good of this or that people—employed only the fame of powers in a mechanical or commercial line—this man might have been as much their superior in opulence as he is now in theology.

It ill becomes a member of Christian society to urge, as an apology for the scanty pittance of a pastor, that he consented to receive such a stipend, when first he settled with his people. Perhaps he did, and it might be enough for his comfortable support then, though it may be that both his family and the experience of living have been doubled since. Where such men rule the affairs of a church, it is a comfort to reflect that "God takes care

---
[30] 1 Corinthians 9:11, 13-14.

for oxen."[31] You, my brethren, know what is necessary to a minister's comfortable and respectable support in this city, and will take care to keep your minister free from any pecuniary embarrassments.

Promote a studious habit in your minister
Secondly, you should be careful not only to allow your minister an adequate support, but must also, as far as possible, withhold yourselves from any intrusions on his time.

Nothing, next to the honor of Christ and the interest of souls is dear to a studious pastor, as time; and a minister who thinks lightly of its value, betrays an ignorance and indolence, which, if indulged, will eventually debase both his character and labors.

A studious habit, as you have heard today, is essential to a stated minister. A lively imagination may serve an itinerant; but when a man becomes stationary, and preaches three or four times a week to the same people, unless he be industrious in furnishing his mind, his services will soon become insipid, void of solidity, fraught with tautology, and unfit for edification. And what is the result? Why, the thoughtful hearers must either abide with dissatisfaction or in grief retire; while the ignorant are kept in their ignorance and remain babes, when under a judicious ministry they might have become "fathers in Christ."[32]

Am I not now speaking to your pastor? No, my brethren, he has had better advice than I can give him. I speak to you. I want to convince you that, for your own sakes, you should promote a studious habit in your minister. Allow him every inch of time he wants. Neither call upon him, nor expect him to call upon you for no better purpose than to gossip. Especially let his mornings and his Saturdays be sacred—it is little short of cruelty to inter-

---

[31] 1 Corinthians 9:9.
[32] 1 Corinthians 4:15.

rupt him then. As you love him, so, no doubt, you will feel a pleasure in his company, but let him choose his own times for seeing you; and do not accuse him of criminal negligence, if his visits are less frequent than you expect. Perhaps at the very moment of your disappointment, he was studying something against the Lord's day for your case—perhaps at the moment that you are censuring him for his neglect, he is wrestling with God for you in his closet!

If a pastor devotes those hours to the theatre, the card table, or the race ground, which ought to be given to his people, God forbid I should become his apologist. However,to apologize for a studious minister, is always just, and often necessary. Such a one, and such only, will answer to the character of the predicted pastor, who should "feed his flock with knowledge and understanding"[33]—the pastor "after God's own heart."[34]

Attendance to the ordinances
Third, if you would improve the gift of a pastor, you must duly attend upon the sacred ordinances that he administers. Without this, your profiting will be hardly possible. Irregular attendance will not only prevent your own improvement; but prove a pernicious example to others, and greatly discourage your minister. Painful indeed, when a man has been laboring a week to get food for the souls of his people, to see them turn their backs upon it when it is set before them; and in effect, pronounce it unworthy their acceptance.

Nor should you only avoid irregular, but late attendance also—a practice as disgraceful to those who are found in it, as it is disturbing to the congregation on which they so unseasonably intrude themselves; and insulting to their Maker, on whose

---

[33] Jeremiah 3:15.
[34] 1 Samuel 13:14.

worship they set so little reverence. The devotees of the world might, if these dilatory attendants on sacred ordinances were not lost to shame, put them to the blush. Look into the places of amusement, my brethren, and long before the bagatelles[35] of the evening being to be exhibited, you will see the seats occupied, and the spectators waiting. O my God! How few, do the ministers of the sanctuary find thus waiting for you! Say, my brethren, is it seemly that the god of this world should glory over the God of heaven; and say, "my worshippers are more faithful than yours!" and will you assist his triumphs?

With a few, a very few exceptions, I will venture to say, that no just apology can be made for this indecent practice. Have you families that require your attendance? Rise but a quarter of an hour sooner, and you will no longer find an inconvenience there. The excuses that are derived from food or dress, are so inconsistent with sincere religion, that to suppose them in a Christian society would be absurd. The man who can neglect the honor of his God, and the interests of his soul, to gratify either the interior or the exterior of his body, wants something more than argument to "turn from idolatry to serve the living and true God."[36]

Farther, public ordinance will be followed with little profit unless you seriously attend to ministerial instruction and devoutly engage in divine worship. How unseemly, during the seasons of prayer or praise, to behold people staring about them with vacant countenances, which betray the lack of devotion of their hearts!

Brethren, I entreat that this may not be the case with you, nor should you merely attend to the devotional parts of the public service, but unite in them. This is not the time for the exercise of a critical taste; nor is the intercourse of a rebel with his God to be

---

[35] *Bagatelles* meaning a short piece of music usually of a light, mellow character.
[36] 1 Thessalonians 1:9.

judged by the rules of ancient or modern oratory. Forget not, my brethren, that such only worship God acceptably, who "worship him in Spirit and in truth."[37]

And, how unseemly for people to be gazing upon the congregation, whispering, smiling, or sleeping, when the messages of salvation are delivered! Is it thus that criminals receive the news of pardon? Is it thus that subjects receive the mandates of their prince? Is it thus that Christians hear the gospel of the Savior? Never, I sincerely trust, will your pastor witness such indecencies in you.

Embrace the truth he delivers

Fourth, you cannot improve the gift of a pastor unless you cordially embrace the truth he delivers, and yield to the just reproofs he may administer, and the Scriptural precepts he may enforce.

Satisfied, as you have this day publicly professed to be with his ministry, it is a warrantable presumption that you consider what he delivers as evangelical truth, but ministerial wisdom and fidelity, require much variety in the mode of repenting and enforcing it. In a congregation of any size, the circumstances of the hearers will greatly vary. One may be living in habits of iniquity while he is carelessly hastening to everlasting burnings. Another may be distressed under recent awakenings. A third may want instruction about coming to Christ. A fourth may be struggling with temptation. A fifth, burdened with heavy affliction. A sixth may be rejoicing in the God of his salvation. A seventh may have defiled his garments, and by some awful crime brought reproach on the religion he professed. Now, amidst this variety, is it possible for a minister, who is "to give to every man his portion of meat in due season,"[38] to be always insisting upon one topic or

---

[37] John 4:24.
[38] Matthew 24:45.

aiming at one character only? And would it not be highly unreasonable for an individual to complain and say, "My minister has neglected me today!" Give your minister for this, that, as he has had the most experience, so he must be the best judge of what is seasonable; and rather water his ministry with your prayers, than blacken it by your complaints.

Should you, my brethren, when your minister is dissecting the human character, discover some darling sin in your bosom, before now concealed from your notice, be not offended at the preacher—he did not put it there. Of yourselves be ashamed—with yourselves be offended—of your own heart say, "It is despicably wicked," but thank the honest man who discovered to you the viper before it gave the mortal bite.

Strange it is that such advice should be necessary, but instances have occurred, and not a few, of persons who have turned most bitter adversaries to their minister. For what? Only "for telling them the truth!"[39] The love of delusion is an ancient feature in the human character. "Prophesy smooth things," said the people, "who would not hear the law of the Lord; prophesy deceits."[40] The false prophets obeyed, and "the blind led the blind, until both fell into the ditch."[41]

There is one reflection, blessed be God! that affords us habitual satisfaction. When we discharge our office with fidelity, we "manifest ourselves to the consciences of men,"[42] although it frequently occasions the loss of their affections. But be assured, my brethren, that whether ministerial fidelity be pleasant or not, it will always be found profitable.

Give me the preacher who opens the folds of my heart; who accuses me, convicts me, and condemns me before God. Give

---

[39] Galatians 4:16.
[40] Isaiah 30:9–10.
[41] Matthew 15:14.
[42] 2 Corinthians 4:2.

Ordination for W. Belsher

me the preacher who loves my soul too well to suffer me to go on in sin, unreproved, through fear of giving me the offence. Give me he who draws the line with accuracy between the delusions of fancy, and the impressions of grace. Give me the shepherd who pursues me from one hiding place to another, until I am driven from every refuge of lies. Give me the preacher who gives me no rest until he sees me, with unfeigned penitence, trembling at the feet of Jesus; and then, and not until then, soothes my anguish, wipes away my tears, and comforts me with the cordials of grace.

Give me the preacher "who constantly affirms that they who have believed, be careful to maintain good works;"[43] who insists that a life of peace and communion with God is utterly abhorrent to the practice of iniquity. Give me him who faithfully reminds me, that "if I sin so that grace may abound, my damnation is just."[44]

Give me the preacher who pants not for my safety only, but also for my increase in grace; who cautions me, "reproves me, rebukes me, exhorts me with all long-suffering and doctrine."[45] Give me the man who charges me "to give all diligence to add to my faith, virtue; and to virtue, knowledge; and to knowledge, temperance; and to temperance, patience; and to patience, godliness; and to godliness, brotherly kindness; and to brotherly kindness, charity."[46] Brethren, if Christ has given you such a man as this, receive him as an angel from heaven,[47] and prize such a pastor as one of the most valuable gifts that can be imparted to the church.

What, are we better than meteors, my brethren, if we only catch the eye of transient admiration? May you find in your pas-

---

[43] Titus 3:8.
[44] Romans 6:1-2.
[45] 2 Timothy 4:2.
[46] 2 Peter 1:5-7.
[47] Galatians 4:14.

tor a more permanent and influential luminary! As the rays of the sun penetrate the frozen earth, loosen the clouds, and call forth the verdure, the beauty, and the fruitfulness of the plant; so, beneath the divine blessing, may the faithful discourses of our brother sink into your hearts, detach them from the embraces of the world, and cause you to be fruitful in every good work.[48]

He who sends his hearer away with mere admiration of the speaker does nothing. He that sends him away with admiration of himself does worse than nothing. But he that sends him away penetrated with conviction, self-accused, self-abhorred, crying for mercy to pardon his guilt, and grace to sanctify his polluted heart—that preacher, or rather God by him, has done much. "He has turned a sinner from the error of his way,"[49] and he "shall be had in everlasting remembrance."[50]

To what end do I make these remarks? For this end, my brethren, that the more faithful your pastor is, the more you honor him as a man of principle, and prize him as one of all men the most likely to do you good.

Resolve to cease with complaint
You will find it necessary, not only to guard yourselves against entertaining any unbecoming sentiments of your minister, but also to discountenance every appearance of it in others. For one complaining, dissatisfied member in a religious society, if encouraged by the rest, will be like the poison in the blood, or the leaven in the meal which secretly but effectually insinuates itself, until the whole mass be contaminated. "Mark them," says the apostle, "who cause divisions among you, and avoid them; for they gratify their own passions, but serve not our Lord Jesus

---

[48] Colossians 1:10.
[49] James 5:20.
[50] Psalm 112:6.

Ordination for W. Belsher

Christ."[51] Such persons will assume the spirit of zeal and pretend concern for truth, but "by their fruits you shall know them;"[52] and when they are discovered, unless they give the sincerest proofs of penitence, let them be put from the church, as the leper from the camp, lest they defile all who come near them.

Reflect, my brethren, of how much importance it is for each one of you to "study the things that make for peace, and the things whereby you may edify one another."[53] What is an unworthy member of a Christian society? What, but a blotch upon the face of beauty—a bramble in a garden of lilies![54] O that each of you may be preserved from disfiguring or disgracing the church of God!

You must not only be concerned to avoid dishonoring the church, but to be growingly ornamental to it. Most justly does the apostle represent one end of ministerial instruction, by the effects of the continual nourishment, and the fostering care of a tender nurse upon the body of a healthy child. Christ, says he, "has given pastors and teachers, that you may grow up to a perfect man—to the measure of the stature of the fulness of Christ."[55] You see, brethren, Christ is the standard of Christian maturity. Before we are "born from above,"[56] we are all in the likeness of the first, the fallen Adam.[57] In regeneration we are formed anew, but we are brought forth babes, and our character is imperfect. Every gradation from a resemblance of the first Adam to the likeness of the second, is adding another cubit to our spiritual stature. Still, we shall never be perfect men until we attain to "the fullness of Christ," and for that we must wait till

---

[51] Romans 16:17-18.
[52] Matthew 7:20.
[53] Romans 14:19.
[54] Song of Songs 2:2.
[55] Ephesians 4:13.
[56] John 3:3.
[57] Romans 5:12-21.

"we see him as he is."[58] In this world there is always room to advance. let us then be going on to perfection, and so receive "the sincere milk of the Word, as to grow thereby."[59] O what a heaven on earth would that church be, all whose members were thus "growing up to the head, even Christ,"[60] or to follow the apostle in a figure of greater boldness, and not less expression:

> forgetting the things that are behind and reaching forth to those which are before, were pressing towards the mark for the prize of their high calling of God, in Christ Jesus![61]

Let Greece pour forth from all her cities to gaze on the Olympian contests—with superior satisfaction would I fix my eyes on such a scene as this; and pointing to the holy company, address each heedless passenger and say, "behold! so run they not as uncertainly—so contend they not as those who beat the air—they strive not for a corruptible crown, but an incorruptible, a crown of righteousness which the Lord, the righteous judge, shall give them in that day."[62] O, my brethren, strive to be the most zealous, the most affectionate, the most holy people in all the world. "Let your profiting appear to all men;"[63] then also shall your teacher with pious transport exclaim, "I have not run in vain, nor labored in vain."[64]

Render him a blessing

The last thing I would recommend to you in order to improve the gift of Christ, is to render him as extensive a blessing as you can. He is given by Christ "to edify," that is, to build the church

---

[58] 1 John 3:2.
[59] 1 Peter 2:2.
[60] Ephesians 4:15.
[61] Philippians 3:13-14.
[62] 1 Corinthians 9:25-26; 2 Timothy 4:8.
[63] 1 Timothy 4:15.
[64] Philippians 2:16.

of God, to put more stones into the sacred edifice that the superstructure may rise until it becomes a complete temple for the Lord.

The enlargement of the church universal is the wish of every Christian, and the increase of a particular Christian society ought to be pursued by each member of it. But see not, my brethren, to augment your congregation at the expense of others. Few that are seduced to a new communion, prove for any length of time a comfort or an honor to it. "Covet not," therefore in this sense, "anything that is your neighbors."[65] Do nothing in relation to another evangelical congregation, which you would not approve in the conduct of that congregation to you. There are, indeed, some cases where the admission of members from other communions is just. But would it not be proper, in such cases, to take no steps whatever until the persons who make the application, be referred to their former minister that he may have an opportunity of serious conversation with them upon the subject before they desert him? Such an open, generous conduct would, I should hope, prevent those party feuds and jealousies which have too often been the disgrace and the torment of Christian societies, whose great aim should have been to "walk in love," and to "strive together for the faith of the gospel."[66]

If we may judge of future affection among the churches of Christ in this city, by the singular circumstances of the present day, we may warmly congratulate you on the opening prospect. It is not a common case for a minister to be ordained over one congregation, in the house belonging to another in the same town. In some instances, indeed, it has not been necessary, but in others, too often the one has been too haughty to ask or the other too unkind to grant. With joy I contemplate all you, my brethren,

---

[65] Exodus 20:17.
[66] Philippians 1:27.

as rising above the government of these unlovely tempers, and most sincerely do I pray that you may ever consider yourselves as members but of one family, though you find it convenient to occupy different apartments.

Where then shall you seek for additions? From where your Lord directs you—from the highways and hedges—from the unawakened, the careless, the profane. By the awakening, the enlightening, the renewing of such as these, seek to build up that part of the church to which you particularly belong. Look into your families—are there none of this description there? Reflect on the character of your neighbors—are there none among them? These are the persons, whom, by every affectionate persuasion, you must "compel to come in, that the Lord's house may be filled."[67]

> Invite the strangers all around
> Your pious march to join,
> And spread the sentiments you feel
> Of faith and love divine.[68]

Encourage your minister in going among the neighboring villages. Get houses opened and registered for him to preach in. Use your influence in bringing persons to hear. Countenance him by your attendance when he makes these evangelical excursions; and when, either at home or abroad, you perceive persons affected under the Word, speak to them, introduce them to the minister, encourage their attendance, comfort them under the persecutions to which they may be exposed for the sake of religion. Should they decidedly appear renewed persons, and be desirous of partaking with you of the privileges of church fellowship, let no unnecessary, no unscriptural delay, prevent their

---

[67] Luke 14:23.
[68] C.M. Doddridge (1702–1751), "Asking the Way to Zion."

admission to the table of the Lord. Thus, will you hold up the hands of your pastor, become blessings both to the church and to the world, and prove that you have not received the gift of Christ in vain.

Finally, "If there be any consolation in Christ; if any fellowship of the Spirit; if any comfort of love; if any bowels and mercies, fulfil your pastor's joy,"[69] that beholding your rapid improvement in every amiable temper and Christian grace, seeing your "love and your zeal abounding yet more and more, in knowledge and all judgment," and yourselves "filled with the fruits of righteousness, which are by Jesus Christ to the glory and praise of God,"[70] he may have increasing reason to join the happy and affectionate apostle in saying, "What is my hope? What is my joy? What is my crown of rejoicing? Are not even you in the presence of the Lord Jesus Christ at his coming?"[71]

---

[69] Philippians 2:1-2.
[70] Philippians 1:9, 11.
[71] 1 Thessalonians 2:19.

10
An Early Acquaintance with the Holy Scriptures[1]

August 13, 1797

"And that from a child you have known the Holy Scriptures, which are able to make you wise to salvation, through faith which is in Christ Jesus." 2 Timothy 3:15

Reverence for divine revelation has been in every period a discriminating characteristic of good men. In the early ages of the Jewish church when, as yet, neither the devotional productions of David, nor the sublime productions of succeeding prophets had enriched the sacred page, "In those days the word of the Lord was precious."[2]

The royal psalmist not only possessed of the writings of Moses, but being also illuminated with the spirit of wisdom, exclaims:

O how I love your law! It is my meditation day and night; I esteem your statutes above gold, yea, more than fine gold; my soul breaks for the longing it has to your judgements at all times: they are sweeter than honey or the honeycomb.[3]

Nor is it a matter of surprise when we reflect that all the moral difference between the king of Israel and the princes of the

---

[1] *An Early Acquaintance with the Holy Scriptures in a Sermon in Behalf of the Walworth Charity and Sunday-Schools for Poor Boys; Preached at Mr. Booth's Meeting-House, Little Prescot-Street, London, August 13, 1797* (London: J. W. Morris, 1800).

[2] 1 Samuel 3:1.

[3] Psalm 119.

heathen, with their respective subjects, arose from this one thing—that the heathen were without any means of religious instruction save the book of nature, and the traditions of their fathers. Even these latter means, flowing through polluted channels age after age, were at length wholly corrupted and, like clouds of darkness, only tended to veil the true knowledge of God rather than faithfully exhibit him.

The Jews however, above all other nations, were chosen to hear his voice, to know his will, and to preserve his truth until the great Prophet of the church should come to lead the nations into all truth. Of this privilege Moses, with peculiar solemnity, reminds the posterity of Abraham:

> For ask now of the days that are past which were before you since the day that God created man upon the earth, and ask from the one side of heaven to the other, whether there has been any such thing as this great thing is, or has been heard like it? Did ever people hear the voice of God speaking out of the midst of the fire as you have heard, and live?[4]

Revelation demonstrated

To form a true idea of the advantages derived from revelation in this infant state, let us only go through the heathen world and mark the worship and manners of different nations. Here you see women (lost to all sense of decency) weeping for Tammuz;[5] there, the beastly group celebrating the accursed orgies of Bacchus. In one place, mothers casting their own children into the arms of a brazen, burning statue of Moloch. In another, the priests of Baal cutting and tearing their own bodies "with lances and knives, and crying 'Oh Baal, hear us!'"[6]

---

[4] Deuteronomy 4:32–33.
[5] Ezekiel 8:14.
[6] 1 Kings. 18:28.

Early Acquaintance with the Holy Scriptures

Now turn your eyes to Jerusalem the city of God, walk about Zion and mark well her solemn rites and songs. No idol deity is seen within her temple and on her altar no human blood is spilt. Unsullied chastity is demanded of her priests and enjoined on all her worshippers. Examine the laws by which their celestial Sovereign rules them and witness their epitome, "You shall love the Lord your God with all your heart, and your neighbor as yourself."[7] And now, judge whether every holy mind had not reason to rejoice in God's testimonies.

When our beloved Savior appeared in the world, though he made so ample a revelation of divine truth, yet he spoke with the highest respect of the Old Testament writings. Constantly did he appeal to them as containing those principles on which his own dispensation was founded, and those predictions of himself which served to demonstrate beyond contradiction the divinity of his mission: "Search the Scriptures (said Jesus). In them you think you have eternal life, and these are they that testify of me."[8]

It is of these Scriptures that the apostle speaks in my text as being known to Timothy from his early years through the advantages of a pious education, for we find by the first chapter that his maternal ancestors for two generations were numbered with the faithful.

In our text, and its connection, the apostle commends the Scriptures to our regard on three accounts:

First, the divinity of their origin: "They are given by the inspiration of God."

Secondly, the purity of their nature: "The holy Scriptures." These, like their divine author, are pure light, and in them is no darkness at all.

---

[7] Deuteronomy 6:5; Luke 10:27.
[8] John 5:39.

Third, their beneficial tendency: "Able to make you wise to salvation."

The satisfaction found in Scripture

It has indeed been questioned as to whether the latter excellency attributed to the Scriptures be justly spoken of since, if the writings of the Old Testament were alone able to make us wise unto salvation, what necessity could there be for the additional books of the New Testament?

This is not a reason for controversy. One remark only I would make, and that is that the apostle connects faith in Christ with a knowledge of the Old Testament: "Through faith which is in Christ Jesus."[9] Now that same faith into which Timothy was initiated, the New Testament also exhibits to us so that we must consider the assertion in the text as relating to the whole revelation of God. The Scriptures of both testaments contain truths which instruct us in the way of salvation.

How great the encomium![10] Here this sacred volume stands unrivalled. Some books may instruct us how to obtain wealth, others may assist us in maintaining or restoring our health, and others may make us wise to secure a reputation, but the Bible alone can make us wise for salvation.

That man is a sinner, and that his sin diminishes his present enjoyment and endangers all his future happiness, every conscience witnesses, but whom did the light of nature ever instruct in the way of salvation? Should we appeal to the ignorant Otaheitan[11] or the uncivilized Hottentot?[12] Or let the inquiry, "What must I do to be saved?" be put even to a civilized or en-

---

[9] Romans 3:22.
[10] *Encomium* meaning writing or speech which praises something or someone highly.
[11] A (then unreached) native of Tahiti.
[12] The nomadic people of Southwest Africa.

Early Acquaintance with the Holy Scriptures

lightened heathen; to a Tully,[13] or a Socrates—what reply could they have given? To a mind conscious of its depravity, burdened with guilt, tortured with fearful apprehensions of almighty indignation, and panting to know whether its crimes might be forgiven, what peace could any of these have administered? It is probable they might conjecture the fact, but what truly awakened sinner can rest his hopes on a basis so precarious?

But from the holy Scriptures we obtain the amplest satisfaction on this important subject. Here heavenly mercy appears with pardon in her hands. Here the God we have offended passes by us proclaiming, "the Lord God, gracious and merciful, slow to anger, pardoning iniquity, transgression and sin."[14]

Here we see a thousand sinners like ourselves successfully pleading for forgiveness, or rejoicing in the mercy they have found:

- "I acknowledged my sin to you, and my iniquity have I not hid. I said, "I will confess my transgressions to the Lord;" and you forgave the iniquity of my sin."[15]
- "Come and hear, all you that fear God, and I will declare what he has done for my soul."[16]
- "Behold, for peace I had great bitterness but you have in love to my soul delivered it from the pit of corruption, for you have cast all my sins behind your back."[17]
- "Another, penetrated with humility and glowing with gratitude, exclaims: 'I was a blasphemer, and a persecutor, and injurious; but I obtained mercy.'"[18]

---

[13] Marcus Tullius Cicero.
[14] Exodus 34:6.
[15] Psalm 32:5.
[16] Psalm 34:4.
[17] Isaiah 38:17.
[18] 1 Timothy 1:13.

In these sacred pages too, we find the God of mercy kindly inviting us, guilty as we are, to "come boldly to a throne of grace so that we may receive mercy, and obtain grace to help in time of need."[19] Here also the curtain that hides the world of glory from our view is drawn aside and, in heaven, we see an innumerable company of happy saints. Once these all were sinners as we are today, but made perfect now both in purity and bliss, now celebrate the mercy of God in everlasting hymns.

And do the Scriptures bring all this to view? Do they lay a foundation on which one so vile as I may securely build my hope of reconciliation to God? Blessed volume! I receive you as the shepherds received the descending angels who brought the glad tidings of a Savior for all people. I receive you "with fear and great joy."[20]

Salvation obtained by Scripture

Nor is this all, but my heart asks another question: "How is this salvation to be obtained?" And the holy Scriptures afford me all the satisfaction that I desire. They not only point out the object, but also put me in the road, and furnish me with supplies while I am "Pressing towards the mark for the prize of my high calling."[21] "I am the way," says Jesus the Son of God, "and no man comes to the Father but by me."[22] And in perfect union with the declarations of the master are those of his inspired servants:

- "This is a faithful saying and worthy of all acceptation, that Christ Jesus came into the world to save sinners."[23]

---

[19] Hebrews 4:16.
[20] Matthew 28:8.
[21] Philippians 3:14.
[22] John 14:6.
[23] 1 Timothy 1:15.

- "By a new and living way which he has consecrated for us, through the veil, that is to say, his flesh."[24]
- "Who was delivered for our offences, and was raised again for our justification."[25]
- "Him has God exalted with his right hand to be a Prince and a Saviour, for to give repentance to Israel, and forgiveness of sins."[26]
- "Having suffered the just for the unjust, to bring us to God."[27]
- "God is just and yet the justifier of the ungodly."[28]

Belief and affection
Still I enquire farther: "How am I to enjoy a sensible participation of the blessings of salvation?" The holy Scriptures say, "He that believes on the Son has everlasting life."[29] They teach me that whoever truly and heartily receives the Lord Jesus, as exhibited in the gospel, as his infallible teacher, atoning priest, and rightful sovereign, so as to believe his doctrine, rely on his mediation, and delight in obedience to his laws, shall be saved.

They also say that no sincere enquirer may be at a loss to judge whether he be personally interested in this salvation or not since the holy Scriptures declare that such a dedication of the soul to God, being accomplished through his gracious influence upon the heart will be attended with such an effectual, universal, and abiding change in the feelings, temper, and conduct, that such an one will be a new creature. Henceforth he will take delight in prayer and other exercises of religion, mourn over his

---
[24] Hebrews 10:20.
[25] Romans 4:25.
[26] Acts 5:31.
[27] 1 Peter 3:8.
[28] Romans 3:26.
[29] John 3:36.

sins before God, be kind and affectionate to his enemies, prefer the society of the Lord's people to that of all other men, and be looking with cheerful expectation for "the blessed hope and glorious appearing of the great God, and our Savior Jesus Christ."[30]

Perseverance enjoyed
Finally, to encourage every humble follower of the Lamb, this sacred volume promises support under every trial and in every duty; preservation by the divine power while on earth, and to crown all at last, the felicity of heaven, consisting in the everlasting deliverance of the soul from ignorance, guilt, misery, and sin; and the body from pain, disease, corruption, and death. All of these shall be enjoyed in the society of holy angels, the whole company of the redeemed, and the Lord Jesus himself, in whose presence there is fullness of joy and at whose right hand there are pleasures forevermore.

Demonstrating how Scripture makes wise
How desirable is the wisdom which comes down from above! How blessed the man whose bosom it illuminates, enraptures, and exalts! All human science must pay homage here. Compared with this, all the intelligence which ever enriched the mind or gave celebrity to the name of man, is but vanity and vexation of spirit, "He that increases knowledge increases sorrow."[31] The fact is as humiliating as it is notorious that after the laborious researches of half a century, the far greater part of our attainments expire with our lives or, in the more expressive language of the apostle, "as for knowledge, it shall vanish away."[32]

But this heavenly wisdom, simple and harmonious, though sublime and profound, both satisfies and abides. Accommodated

---

[30] Titus 2:13.
[31] Ecclesiastes 1:18.
[32] 1 Corinthians 13:8.

Early Acquaintance with the Holy Scriptures

to the capacity of the babe in Christ, and yet fraught with a grandeur and a majesty which command the reverence of the profoundest scholar, constrains the simplest disciple to love, and the aged apostle to exclaim, "I count all things but loss and dung for the excellency of the knowledge of Christ Jesus my Lord."[33]

Neither the labors of the historian, the skill of the grammarian, the penetration of the philosopher, nor the acumen of the logician are necessary here. Approach, you humble peasants! You unlettered artificers, draw near! Though destitute of literacy advantages, unskilled in the cumbrous volumes of antiquity, unacquainted with the effusions of modern times, and strangers to all that confers the laurel on the student's brow, even you may learn from the Bible to be "wise to salvation."

It is true, you may meet with prophecies which you may not be able to unfold, and allusions which you are not able to illustrate; but know that as it concerns salvation, the knowledge of these is not essential. The truth you are to learn and the precepts you are to obey are so legible that "he who runs may read;"[34] and so easy that a wayfaring man, though a fool, shall not err essentially in understanding them. One thing alone is necessary for all, and that is that we "must be converted and become as little children,"[35] before we can understand the things of the kingdom of God. That simplicity of mind which is the offspring of genuine humility is all you want. Without this, the philosopher remains (as to the religion of Jesus) a fool; but with it, the most ignorant enquirer shall be made "wise to salvation."[36]

---

[33] Philippians 3:8.
[34] Habakkuk 2:2.
[35] Matthew 13:3.
[36] 2 Timothy 3:15.

Selected Works of Samuel Pearce

Scripture is necessary for youth

Yet, easy as the acquisition of this wisdom may be, it is not limited in its duration, nor feeble in its influence. As the benevolent institution of Sunday schools, whereby children the most ignorant and wretched are prepared for activity and usefulness in maturer years, so the knowledge of the Scriptures is preparatory both to a life of goodness, and a heaven of blessedness. The very truths which are revealed by the Scriptures now will be the subject of our sweetest meditations and loudest songs in the heavenly world and—pardon so humble an allusion—the alphabet we learn in time shall assist us in reading the lessons of eternity.

Who then can begin to acquire this sacred knowledge too soon? It was the privilege of Timothy that, "from a child he had known the holy Scriptures."[37] Blessed are the children whose infant minds, like his, are thus illuminated, and blessed are all those who contribute to this salutary illumination!

"To everything, (says Solomon) there is a season,"[38] and surely the time of youth is the best and most proper season to form an acquaintance with the holy Scriptures. Everybody knows that the earliest impressions which the mind receives are the most permanent and influential. Proof of this each of us has in his own recollection and may observe in the world at large by only comparing the present prejudices of men with their respective education. Why is it that so many are at this moment zealous for the religion of Mohammed? Is it not because they were taught from their childhood to venerate the Koran? And would not these have been equally attached to Judaism, had they been educated Jews? Or to paganism, had they been brought up with the pagans? In our own country do we not see that, in general, children are prejudiced in favour of the opinions of their fathers?

---

[37] 2 Timothy 3:5.
[38] Ecclesiastes 3:1.

Early Acquaintance with the Holy Scriptures

Even if, upon conviction, anyone recedes from the denomination of his family, is it not with a degree of reluctance?

How careful then should we be that the first notions of religion which our children form should be agreeable to the truth as it is in Jesus. And how is it possible to accomplish so noble and important an end without leading them to an acquaintance with the holy Scriptures, so they may be secured both from the plausible insinuations of the infidel, and the vicious seductions of the licentious in future years?

To the want of this pious care must, in some respects, be attributed that profaneness, sabbath breaking, dishonesty, lewdness, and those other vices which characterize and disgrace the present times. In days when parents and guardians were not wanting in the duty of Scriptural instruction, England had not such crimes so largely to answer for to God. When we as a people resume these important attentions to the rising generation, the happy fruits will doubtless be soon visible in a general reformation of our corrupted manners.

Scripture calls for universal instruction

The influence of a Scriptural education extends to all the stages, relations, and circumstances of human life and, like the meandering stream, fertilize every part through which it flows. It forms the mind for the discharge of social and domestic duties, since here the child learns to "obey his parents in all things because it is right in the Lord."[39] And, when providence shall put him in a parent's place, he will be fitted to govern as well as obey. Here the servant is taught diligence, submission, cheerful obedience, and inviolable fidelity to his master and, should he ever be a master himself, to deal kindly and justly by those who serve him. In short, the holy Scriptures are calculated for uni-

---

[39] Ephesians 6:1.

versal "instruction in righteousness, that the man of God may be thoroughly furnished to all good works."[40]

I scarcely need to observe that pious education is needed to secure good order in a body politic, or in civil life. "This age," says one, "has had notorious evidence of the dreadful barbarism into which an ignorant multitude, unaccustomed to the use and the knowledge of the Scriptures, may be readily plunged." Recall the horrid scenes of the year eighty in this metropolis, and of ninety-one in Birmingham. Here see a lawless herd composed of our own countrymen and neighbors committing acts the most violent and base! Who of us can remember the houses of respectable citizens in flames and the houses erected for the worship of God in ruins during the transaction of those infamous scenes by a mob? Who can recall such minds who, not stored with sacred knowledge in childhood, were ready to perform such infernal projects in their rising years? And who would not endeavor by every possible means to season the minds of the rising generation with pious instruction as shall dispose them at once to execrate the conduct of their ancestors, and secure them from treading in the steps?

In large towns like this, it should seem of greater importance to the public tranquility that children be principled in religion and virtue, than in smaller ones. So depraved is the human heart, that it is far more susceptible of evil than of good impressions. And not only every bad man, but every wicked child has his circle of influence: now mingling, as youth of both sexes do in this populous city, an individual of a corrupted mind may be highly influenced by the morals of the rest—but what if the bulk be corrupt! How much do those around them need to have their minds fortified to resist the effect of their sinful discourse and pernicious example? And is it possible to accomplish this better

---

[40] 2 Timothy 3:17.

than by an early initiation into the knowledge of the holy Scriptures?

If we suffer their minds to remain unacquainted with their duty, both to God and their neighbor, let us not expect that we shall be able to repel the charge which a future day may bring against us, that to us belongs at least one half of the guilt and shame of all the depredations and miseries that may follow other riots—perhaps even more dreadful than the former.

The necessity of Scripture in society

The friends of despotism indeed may oppose the instruction of the poor and contend that mental improvement is inimical to due subordination. To glance at the Bible, however, is to see such unworthy reasoning subject of the state by learning to revere the powers that be as the ordinance of God. Shall I become a worse member of society by forming an acquaintance with that book which directs me to, "Love my neighbor as myself; to forgive injuries; to do good, and communicate; to bless them that curse me, and to overcome evil with good?"

This is not Christian patriotism. It may agree with the views of the prophet of Arabia or of the high-priest of Rome but accords neither with the dictates of right reason, nor the enlarged scheme of Christian philanthropy. "Go, preach my gospel to the poor," said the Son of God; and "suffer the little children to come to me, and forbid them not."[41] Nor does that person act like a philanthropist, nor a disciple of Christ, who would draw a veil over the Sun of Righteousness and, through pride of learning or lust of power, hide the sacred page from human observation.

Deprive a poor man of his Bible and what upon earth has he left to support him under his labor, and console him amidst the sorrows of life? Compare together two men of equal years and

---

[41] Matthew 19:14.

circumstances—the one who has been made wise to salvation while the other remains uninstructed in the sacred page. Now conceive them both, either through sickness or age, detained from the usual labours and enjoyments of life. How different are their feelings in afflictive solitude! To the one, "light arises in darkness."[42] I hear him sing, "Though the fig tree does not blossom, and there be no fruit in the vine;[43] though I walk in the darkness and pass through the valley of the shadow of death, I will fear no evil,[44] but rejoice in the Lord, and joy in the God of my salvation.[45] All things are working together for my good.[46] Wisdom and mercy direct all these dispensations, and him who is infinite in both I humbly call my Father: he promises to give my strength equal to my days; to be with me in every trial; never to leave me nor forsake me; to guide me by his counsel, and then receive me to glory. My flesh and my heart may fail, but God is the strength of my heart, and my portion forever.[47]" Happy man, it is good for you to be afflicted! But tell me, where is this strong consolation? From what sources are your supports derived? Surely, he shall respond, "This is my comfort in my affliction, God's word has quickened me."[48]

What a gloomy contrast, my brethren, does the ignorant child of sorrow present to our view! To him the spring of consolation is sealed and he knows not the hand that visits him. The love of life and fear of death torment his spirit and accelerate the progress of his misery; the dread of an hereafter, for which he is unprepared, distracts him; all earthly pleasures fail him, past sins stare him in the face, unaccompanied with any hope of for-

---

[42] Psalm 112:4.
[43] Habakkuk 3:17.
[44] Psalm 23:4.
[45] Habakkuk 3:18.
[46] Romans 8:28.
[47] Psalms 73:26.
[48] Psalm 119:50.

Early Acquaintance with the Holy Scriptures

giveness; he knows not God, nor Jesus Christ whom he has sent; apprehensions the most gloomy prey upon his heart till at length, he sinks down in despair, and anticipates the reward of his transgressions before he actually receives it. Miserable man, how calamitous your lot! My heart bleeds for you. "Oh if you had known the things that make for the peace; but now they are hid from your eyes! God be merciful to us, and bless us; and cause his face to shine upon us; that your way may be known upon earth, your saving health among all nations. Let the people praise you, O God; let all the people praise you."

Scripture exemplified in youth

In the Scriptural accounts of persons whom God designed for special service, it is remarkable that many of them were prepared for it in their youth. Thus Moses, the illustrious leader of the Israelite host, was trained from a child in the Egyptian court, and so fitted for the public character which he afterwards received. So Samuel, that venerable and disinterested prophet of the Lord, was during his childhood consecrated to Jehovah, and received an early initiation to the services of the sanctuary. Jeremiah was "sanctified from the womb,"[49] and Timothy, the colleague of an apostle, "from a child had known the holy Scriptures."[50]

It must be owned that the youth of Great Britain have had singular advantages for early information. So far back as the ninth century, the justly celebrated Alfred, it is said, founded public schools; and as the whole land at that time lay in profoundest ignorance so that parents, unacquainted with the advantages of instruction, might be supposed indifferent to the education of their children, this wise legislator, with truly paternal benevolence, enacted a salutary law, whereby citizens, at least of

---

[49] Jeremiah 1:5.
[50] 2 Timothy 3:15.

a certain class were obliged to send their children for public tuition. But the state of the times was not favourable to the preservation of an institution so happily established. It was for the interest of the clergy to keep the people in ignorance, and, by preventing their personal acquaintance with the Scriptures, make them dependent on those whose luxurious tables, and increasing treasures, proved the policy of their system of darkness.

Sunday Schools

However, when it pleased God so far to reform the corruptions of the Christian church as to abolish popery in the land, the means of religious information were friends to knowledge; then schools were multiplied, and wisdom increased. From that time to the present, considerate attention has been given to youthful instruction, except amongst the children of the poorest class, who unable to satisfy the demands of a tutor, or to dispense with the trifling fruits of their children's labor, were precluded from participating in the spreading benefit. This was true until gracious heaven first put it into the heart of man to establish Sunday schools; these institutions being supported with no expense to the parent, and only demanding the child's attendance on the Lord's day, diminish nothing from his earnings in the week. Here, religious instruction is imparted; beside which, the day of God is kept from profanation, and care taken that divine worship is duly frequented.

By this institution, thousands, who in all probability must otherwise have lived and died in almost savage ignorance, have been prepared for useful and respectable situations in the civil life, while the hearts of many children have, through the divine blessing following the instructions given them, been impregnated with the seeds of piety, which in a more mature age have produced the fruits of righteousness to the glory of God

Early Acquaintance with the Holy Scriptures

But the institution for which I plead, and to support which you are here assembled, not only provides a Sunday school, which, with literally unlimited benevolence, sets no bounds to number, but invites to instruction the children of all the poor in the vicinity, and also provides for twenty poor boys, as a parent provides for his offspring; or as our heavenly father provides for us all—it provides them not only with instruction for the minds, but raiment for their bodies also. Generous institution! Our hearts are constrained to admiration, and our hands, I trust, will give you ample aid.

Four years ago, this society first sprung into being chiefly by the exertions of that valuable and lamented minister of Jesus Christ, the late Mr. Joseph Swain.[51] He with some others of liberal heart, had long perceived the necessity of an institution of this nature in a neighborhood abounding with poor, and enveloped in ignorance. Great have been the exertions of charity on behalf of this school, which, as you will all readily allow, the most economical management cannot support at a less expense than sixty pounds per annum. It was begun, and at first maintained by private subscriptions, but the necessities of some having compelled them to withdraw their contributions. Providence having removed others, at present little more than half can be depended on: and for the rest we apply you. Yes, in the name of all these lads, and in the name of society at large, to whom each one will prove a blessing or a bane, we appeal to you. Is there a heart so stoical as not to feel? Is there a hand so mercenary as not to give?

Conviction stirred for the work of instructing youth

Soon must these children mingle with the world. Shall they be introduced, as from a den of wild beasts to annoy, or as a flock of harmless sheep to benefit mankind? Shall the pains which have

---

[51] Joseph Swain (1761-1796).

already been taken with them be lost for want of means to repeat them? Shall the opening genius of these lads be nipped in the bud? Shall their parents who look forward to the time, when, detained by infirmity from the sanctuary of God, these their children shall read to them the holy Scriptures—their only consolation in the afflictive hour. Shall these be disappointed? Ah, no, I bode better things. Already you have formed the pious resolution, (and heaven approves it) that having found so good a thing to do today, you will do it with all your might, and liberally encourage an institution which, smiling in its infancy, promises abundant good to society in future years.

Sweet are the works of mercy! Oh, what avails it that you are clothed in purple and fine linen, and fare sumptuously every day, if your bosoms remain strangers to the best of joys—the joys of doing good?

A great philanthropist and popular writer once exclaimed:

> If I may but flatter myself that I have wiped away the tears from the eyes of but one unfortunate fellow creature, such a reflection would wipe away my own in my dying moments.[52]

You, my brethren have now an opportunity for a work even superior in benevolence to wiping the tear of misery away. You may keep it from being shed by many an eye, and by the means of preventing the torments of guilt in many a heart. While by these efforts of kindness you embalm your memories in the hearts of the youth, whose minds you inform, whose morals you improve, and whose happiness you augment. Yes, when the names of slaughtering conquerors shall be no more admired, but held in universal detestation; and when the memorial of the mere wealthy shall be remembered with affectionate respect; altars

---

[52] Jean Bernardin de St. Pierre (1737–1814).

Early Acquaintance with the Holy Scriptures

shall be erected to their virtues; children shall be taught to respect their names, and lisp out their praise; and distant generations shall weep that their faces are seen on earth no more. Partial as is our recover from the illusions of ages when opulence and dominion monopolized respect, we, notwithstanding, find the general sentiment in favour of moral character. Does the mind seek for honor? She finds it in uprightness. Does she enquire for delight? She finds it in benevolence. Ambition is prostrated, and goodness is exalted to the shrine. Your bosoms, brethren, echo to my voice; your feelings justify my assertions.

I tell you of Alexander, the wonder of ages, the conqueror of nations, but like most other children of ambition, the butcher of his brother man!—Alexander is dead! Who amongst you becomes his mourner? What heart heaves for him the sigh? What eye drops for him the tear? But Howard! Thy name kindles in every virtuous bosom sensation of affection, astonishment, and regret; your goodness (how diffusive! Blessed philanthropist!) You need not for a monument to perpetuate your memory. Far as your name is known it is inscribed in the heart of every friend of man!

But why do I speak of the approbation of creatures? Behold the judge of the universe upon his throne. See all nations assembled before him. Hear the sentence that shall eternally fix the states of men, and learn from it the importance of Christian benevolence:

> Then shall the King say to them on his right hand, "Come, you blessed of my Father, inherit the kingdom prepared for you from the foundation of the world: For I was an hungry, and you gave me meat: I was thirsty, and you gave me drink: I was a stranger, and you took me in: Naked, and you clothed me: I was sick, and you visited me: I was in prison, and you came to me." Then shall the righteous answer him, saying, "Lord, when saw we you hungry, and

fed you? or thirsty, and gave you drink? When saw we you a stranger, and took you in? or naked, and clothed you? Or when saw we you sick, or in prison, and came to you?" And the King shall answer and say to them, "Verily I say to you, inasmuch as you have done it to one of the least of these my brethren, you have done it to me."[53]

Concluding remarks

My dear children, hearken! If you should, after all, prove indolent, disobedient, or unthankful. If the knowledge communicated to you should only render you more expert in the service of Satan, of what account will all these benevolent exertions be to you? They will only heighten your guilt, and augment your misery. The holy Scriptures are doubtless and invaluable treasure, and it is the desire of your friends to impart to you the key of knowledge. But if it should prove a price in the hand of those who have no heart to get wisdom, though we may enjoy a satisfaction in having done our best, what will become of you? The Scriptures are not otherwise able to make you wise unto salvation than through faith which is in Christ Jesus. Oh, believe in his name, and love him in sincerity! Then will you continue to carry on those labours of love towards other poor children when we are in our graces. And when it shall please God to remove you from the present scene of action, you will meet us before the throne and enter with us into the joy of the Lord.

Friends and benefactors! We shall meet these children in another world. We shall see some of them, I hope, among the followers of the Lamb. If so, we shall hear them bless God for having given them the Holy Scriptures, and the means of understanding them. And should we also be of that happy company, the remembrance of having been instru-

---

[53] Matthew 25:34–40.

Early Acquaintance with the Holy Scriptures

mental in their salvation, will add to the numerous sources of our enjoyment. But let us take heed, lest while we have contributed to make others wise to salvation through faith which is in Christ Jesus, we ourselves should have our portion with the unbelievers. If unhappiness could have place in heaven, surely it would be in the heart of a child saved by means of early instruction, who should see his instructor lost![54]

---

[54] This institution, since August 1797, when Mr. Pearce so ably pleaded for it, has received such aid from occasional collections at charity sermons, and from new annual subscribers, as to enable it to increase the number of children in each of the schools. There are now in the day-school thirty who are not only educated, but annually clothed; and in the Sunday-school upwards of fifty who are regularly instructed by some of the managers. The increase of the schools rendered it necessary to procure a larger school room; and the society, thinking it desirable to provide, at the same time, a residence for the master, purchased a house in East street, Walworth, and vested it in the hands of twelve trustees, in May 1799; to which they have added a convenient school-room. The expenses hereby incurred have been generously defrayed by the liberality of the public.

11
Motives of Gratitude[1]

November 29, 1798

"And one of them, when he saw that he was healed, turned back and with a loud voice glorified God and fell down at his feet giving him thanks; and he was a Samaritan."
Luke 17:15–16

Some parts of human conduct are so trifling and unworthy that the serious mind feels a mixture of pity and contempt when they come beneath its notice. Other parts are so base and detestable that they furnish matter for the deepest lamentation and regret. While others are so just, so beneficial, or so amiable, that it is impossible to contemplate them without pleasing admiration.

Such are the effusions of a grateful heart. A heart suitably affected with the kindness it has received from another, and expressing, to the utmost reach of language and conduct, its sense of obligation to its benefactor.

The Bible abounds with fine and striking specimens of this lovely temper; and few are more interesting than that presented to us by our text. We read, "as [Jesus] entered into a certain village, there met him ten men that were lepers, who stood afar off" (Luke 17:12).

You may recollect that the Jewish law prohibited leprous persons from abiding in cities or towns[2] so that they were

---

[1] *Motives to Gratitute, A sermon delivered to the Baptist congregation, meeting in Cannon-Street*, Birmingham; *On occasion of the public thanksgiving*. Thursday, November 29, 1798 (Birmingham: Belcher/London: Button, Matthews, and Knott, 1798). This sermon is Pearce's last before his death on October 10, 1799.

[2] Leviticus 13:46.

obliged to retire to the villages, or less populous parts of the country, and being shut out from other society, they formed little parties of their own and passed their time together. It seems one of these was a Samaritan between whose countrymen and the Jews there were no dealings ordinarily; but their common affliction had, in this instance, suspended the effect of party animosity.

Not presuming to come near, lest they should spread the infection, they stood afar off and, "they lift up their voices and said, 'Jesus, master, have mercy on us'" (Luke 17:13).

It is probable that they had heard of his fame "who went about doing good, healing all manner of sickness, and all manner of disease among the people,"[3] and were therefore encouraged to make application to him for personal relief. Surely they could not have applied to one whose power, or whose kindness, would better justify a hope of success, as the issue proves; for he said, "Go, show yourselves to the priests" (Luke 17:14). This injunction contained a pretty strong intimation that he would work a cure; because the Levitical law directed that when a leper was cleansed, he should go and show himself to the priest from whom also he was to receive a certificate of his cleansing[4] in order to his re-admission to social privileges. And it was easy for these lepers to infer that Jesus would not have sent them to the priest had he not intended to make them whole. In adopting this language, it probably was our Lord's design to teach them that to enjoy his blessing they must do his will; and they found their privilege in their obedience, for "as they went they were cleansed" (Luke 17:14).

He who was a Samaritan, our text tells us, was so affected with this sudden display of divine grace and power that both the

---

[3] Matthew 4:23.
[4] Leviticus 14:2.

Motives of Gratitude

testimony of the priest, and the consequent satisfaction he must feel in making use of that testimony, as an introduction to society from which he had perhaps been long expelled, were less to him than the pleasures of gratitude. He hastens to the presence of his deliverer, glorifies God aloud, falls down at Immanuel's feet, and from the fullness of his heart gives him the most affectionate thanks.

Many circumstances combine to render this scene highly interesting. His national character as a Samaritan, the dreadful nature of the complaint from which he had been freed, the sudden and unexpected manner in which it was accomplished, the warmth of his gratitude, and the humble manner in which he expressed it—all affect the heart. But the concluding part of the narrative commands sensations which though of an opposite nature are equally interesting. Jesus said, "were there not ten cleansed? but where are the nine? There are not found that returned to give glory to God save this stranger" (Luke 17:17-18).

Who is there that withholds a censure from these ungrateful lepers? Alas! that censure will more or less involve us all. These men were so eager to enjoy the gift that they forgot the giver; and who among us can boast exemption from the same iniquity! We are all constantly receiving proofs of the bounty of our God. It is his air that we breathe. It is his light that we enjoy. Everything which contributes to our security, our support, or our enjoyment. The heavens, the earth, and universal nature, all conspiring to promote our happiness, bear witness to his beneficence, and loudly demand our grateful acknowledgments; but we too often intent on nothing but our personal safety and comfort, and almost, or wholly unmindful of "the Father of lights, from whom every good and perfect gift comes,"[5] give occasion to the affecting exclamation, "Where are the nine?"

---

[5] Esther 10:3.

In what a base and unworthy light does ingratitude appear when contrasted with the conduct of the grateful leper? And how does the conduct of this man, by all so much approved, recommend itself to universal imitation! What you all admire, I wish you all to become; and to that end I would endeavour to excite your gratitude to God for the benefits you enjoy as men, as Christians, and as Britons.

Our good Creator has demands upon us for ardent gratitude

How capable of happiness has he formed us. Every sense is a distinct avenue to enjoyment. And how many objects to meet and gratify our senses crowd around? All the infinite diversities of form, and of colour, of odour, of taste, and of sound are designed, directly or indirectly, to administer to the comfort of man. For him the sun with all his genial influence rises on our world. For him the moon imparts her light. For him the cattle, the fishes, and the fowl multiply; and to subserve his interests, the prolific earth yields her increase of trees, and herbs, and flowers, "from the cedar of Lebanon to the hyssop that springs out of the wall."[6] Tis be:

> for whom the whole creation smiles,
> At once, the head, the heart, the mouth of all[7]

Man is distinguished above all other beings in the world by his intellectual powers which essentially differ from mere animal instinct, and thereby exalt his nature unspeakably above that of "the brutes which perish." It is through these rational faculties that man is enabled to advance in science and improve in art. What other animals are when they attain to their full growth that, unless it be in mere gesticulation, they are till they die; but

---

[6] 1 Kings 4:33.
[7] James Thomson (1700–1748), "A Hymn on the Seasons."

Motives of Gratitude

man is enabled by observation, reading, conversation, reflection, and experiment, to go on towards perfection; and he who is born a babe may die a Newton. It is this which renders occasional retirement so full of charms to the man of contemplation and virtue while every object in nature, and every event in providence, supplies him with a new theme for profitable meditation. It is this which renders society so sweet and improving while mind unfolds itself to mind, and each individual in the circle participates of the common stock of information. Without this rational faculty we should be wholly incapable of religious exercises. Religion is in fact an abstract thing because its object is invisible. Man alone, amidst all the animal tenants of the globe, can conceive of property distinct from form and space; he alone, therefore, can be devout. The spirit which Jehovah at first breathed into him, pants to find its author and rises in quest of God; and when the longing soul attains to an acquaintance with the deity, there it takes up its everlasting rest; and solacing itself in the divine embrace, with filial feeling, cries, "Whom have I in heaven but you, and there is none upon the earth I desire beside you! My flesh and my heart fail; but God is the strength of my heart, and my portion forever."[8]

To improve our sense of obligation, let us review the conduct of divine providence towards us from the days of helpless infancy to the present hour. How has his hand supplied and his arm sustained us? With what tender and constant care has he watched over us? From what unnumbered evils has he saved us? And with what various and important favours has he enriched us? And all this while we were either too young to reflect upon his goodness, or so abominably ungrateful as to refuse to celebrate it. Have we not on the contrary indulged a thoughtless, trifling, endeavour, and impious spirit? Have we not lived in the habitual

---

[8] Psalm 73:25–26.

neglect of prayer and praise? Have we not said in our hearts, when brought by custom to the ordinances of God's house, "What a weariness is it when will his sabbaths be over!" Yes, have not some broken through the restraints of conscience and education to take their carnal pleasure on God's holy day? How many gracious calls, and solemn warnings have we flighted! How many seasons of improvement wasted and abused! And yet he spares us—yet supports us—yet crowns us with loving kindness and tender mercies! O, while he is thus passing by us, and proclaiming his name, "The Lord, the Lord God, gracious and merciful, slow to anger, and of great kindness."[9] May we feel the strings of our gratitude effectually touched till every power bursts forth in unison, and the grateful song which first sounded on the hill of Zion be resounded throughout the tribes of man: "Bless the Lord, O my soul, and all that is within me, bless his holy name! bless the Lord, O my soul, and forget not all his benefits!"[10]

Obligations for men are greater for Christians

Christianity is a system of truth, goodness, and joy. Like its benevolent author, it is "full of grace."[11] It is here that God displays the riches of his mercy, and the greatness of his love.[12] It breathes "peace and good-will to men."[13] It enlightens by its doctrines. It consolates and cheers by its promises. It purifies by its influence; it displays the duties of the man, the privileges of the Christian. And with prospects the most exalted and refined, animates the breasts of all its true disciples.

---

[9] Exodus 34:6; Psalm 145:8.
[10] Psalm 103:1–2.
[11] John 1:14.
[12] Ephesians 2:4–7.
[13] Luke 2:14.

Motives of Gratitude

The excellency of the religion of Jesus can perhaps be no better illustrated than by comparing it with those which were and still are practiced among the nations who have not been favoured with a revelation from God, "The world knew not God, nor glorified him as God."[14] While in other sciences they advanced, in the science of the Deity their motion was retrograde.[15] For the longer they lived, the more ignorant and evil they became; until, in the expressive language of one who knew them well, "Professing themselves wise they became fools, and their foolish heart was darkened."[16] The history of their worship, which still remains, justifies these assertions; nor is it possible to pursue the narrative of their puerile, wanton, and debauched observances, without astonishment, disgust, and horror. Let Athens, the pride of Greece—famed for knowledge and refinement, producing not only illustrious warriors, but eloquent orators, and renowned philosophers—let Athens teach us the worship of the Gentiles: "There in that polished city, said a witness of unquestionable probity have I seen all the inhabitants (more than thirty thousand) drunk at once,"[17] in honor of the god of wine! With shameless faces they indulged at their religious festivals, the most unlawful passions, and accounted themselves the better saints in proportion to their excessive debaucheries! But, see my brethren, wherever the light of Christ has diffused its rays, these deeds of darkness are no more. And so abhorrent from the gospel is the practice of iniquity that he who avows himself a friend to sin is compelled, if he would be consistent, to avow himself also an enemy to Christianity.

Christianity has been justly styled, "a religion for sinners." Such was the account its blessed author gave of it, and therefore

---

[14] Romans 1:2.
[15] *Retrograde* meaning moving backward.
[16] Romans 1:22.
[17] Plato, in Charles Rollin, *Ancient History*, XII: I. § a.

it is a religion fit for man who has revolted from his allegiance to God, cherished a disaffection to him in his heart, and in instances innumerable has discovered his enmity "by wicked works."

There has never yet been a sinner in the world, who seriously and impartially considered his guilt with its causes and consequences, but has been greatly alarmed, lest the Omnipotent whom he has insulted should punish him for his crimes; and hence the enquiry, in various forms has been anxiously made, "What must I do to be saved?"[18] The concurrent voice of all the tribes of man assert the necessary connection which subsists between natural and moral evil, or that pain is the inevitable consequence of sin. Nor less general has been the hope that vicarious punishment, or one being suffering in the room of another, would be admitted by the judge of the universe. Hence, in all ages have victims bled on the altars; and however the heathen nations differed from each other as to the deities whom they worshipped, or the circumstances of the rites with which they worshipped them, they all acted on this one principle—that without a substituted victim the sinner must personally undergo the deserved punishment. At first the most perfect animals were selected from the flock, or the herd; but at length, apprehensive that these might be inadequate "to take away sin;" and "oppressed by their malady, mankind never rested till they had got to that which they conceived to be the most precious of all—a human sacrifice!" This practice prevailed in every nation under heaven, of which we have received any ancient account. The Egyptians had it in the early part of their monarchy. The Cretans likewise had it, and retained it for a longer time. The nations of Aralia did the same. The people of Dumah in particular, sacrificed every year a child, and buried it underneath an altar which they made use of instead of an idol. The Persians buried people

---

[18] Acts 16:30.

Motives of Gratitude

alive. Amestris, the wife of Xerxes, entombed twelve persons quick underground for the good of her soul. It would be endless to enumerate every city or every province where these dire practices obtained. The Cyprians, the Rhodians, the Phoceans, the Ionians, those of Chios, Lesbos, Tenedos, all had human sacrifices. The natives of the Tauric Chersonesus offered up to Diana every stranger whom chance threw upon their coast. The Romans were accustomed to the like sacrifices. The Gauls and the Germans were so devoted to this shocking custom that no business of any moment was transacted among them without being prefaced with the blood of men. These practices prevailed among all the people of the North, of whatever denomination their chief Gods Thor and Woden were,[19] they thought they could never sufficiently glut with blood. The like custom prevailed to a great degree in Mexico, and in most parts of America. In Africa it is still kept up. The same abominable worship is likewise practiced occasionally in the Islands visited by Captain Cook, and other circumnavigators in the South Sea.

Among the nations of Canaan, the victims were peculiarly chosen, estimating the efficacy of the sacrifice by the dignity of the subject. Their own children, and whatever was nearest and dearest to them, were deemed the worthiest offerings to their God. There were particular children brought up for the altar, as sheep are fattened for the shambles; and they were bought and butchered in the same manner. Those who were sacrificed to Kronus, or Moloch, were thrown into the arms of a molten idol, which stood in the midst of a large fire, and was red with heat. The arms of it were stretched out, with the hands turned upwards, as it were to receive them; yet, sloping downwards, so that they dropped from there into a glowing furnace below. These were the customs which the Israelites learned of the peo-

---

[19] From whom Thurs or Thors-day, and Wednes, or Wodens-day, are named.

ple of Canaan, and for which they are upbraided by the Psalmist: "They sacrificed their sons and their daughters to devils—to the idols of Canaan" (Ps. 106:37-38).

Amidst these abominable cruelties, practiced in the awful name of God, lo! Christianity lifts up her voice, and calling to all the mistaken nations, cries, "Deliver your fellow creatures from going down to the pit. Save them from the immolating knife, or torturing flame, I have found a ransom. God has laid help upon one mighty to save—Jesus, his immaculate son, dies in the room of guilty men—he, by one offering perfected forever them that are sanctified; wherefore be it known to you all, that through this Jesus is preached to you the forgiveness of sins."

Such is the way of peace, revealed in the religion of Jesus. It admits the justice of the principle, which probably, handed down by tradition from the earliest age, the nations had so generally adopted; but, rejecting all their uncommanded victims, it exhibits a sacrifice "Of nobler name, and richer blood than they." It teaches the great mystery of godliness, God manifest in the flesh, for the purpose of our salvation; declaring that Jesus "died, the just for the unjust, that he might bring us to God."[20]

Now this, as far as we can conceive, is the highest act of benevolence that ever engaged the attention of the universe. Our Lord speaks of it in terms, which because they are indefinite, are therefore of so much stronger import, saying, "God so loved the world, that he gave his only begotten son"[21] to save sinners who believe. And indeed, a transaction so new yet so marked with love and mercy—a plan so well adapted to secure all the perfections of the deity from dishonour, while it gives equal solidity to the believing sinner's hopes, must create new views, and new feelings, throughout all the vast dominions of Jehovah wherever

---

[20] 1 Peter 3:18.
[21] John 3:16.

Motives of Gratitude

it is published, understood, and believed. Angels are spoken of as now prying into this mystery of incarnate love, and as finally joining with the redeemed in heaven, who celebrate the mediatorial glories of our Lord the Lamb. And shall we remain unmoved, uninterested, ungrateful? Forbid it, O God of Salvation!

> Praise the Lord! Praise God in the sanctuary. Kings of the earth and all people, princes and all judges of the earth. Both young men and maidens, old men and children. Let them praise the name of the Lord—who has raised up a horn of salvation. Praise the Lord.[22]

Hard, hard as that heart must be which remains insensate amidst these melting of divine compassion—this exuberance of the bounty of a God, need I go without these walls to find such as have often heard the love of God in Christ Jesus read to them from the Scriptures, and declared from the pulpit without any emotions but of weariness and disgust! Blessed be God, the religion of Jesus makes provision also for the conquest of the rebellious heart! When our Lord ascended on high, he sent forth his Holy Spirit, to renovate, subdue, and sanctify the objects of his love. Of this Spirit are all Christians made partakers; so that each saint from experience can say, "The tabernacle of God is with men, and he does dwell among them."[23]

Of this Spirit have we been made partakers? Surely this is an additional motive to our gratitude. Has Jesus healed us of the leprosy of sin? O let us, with the leper, turn back today—let us fall at his feet—let us give him thanks—and glorify God "who gives such power to men."

I might here remind you of the important privileges you enjoy in freedom of access to God; the endearing paternal relation in

---

[22] Psalm 148.
[23] Revelation 21:3.

which he stands to you; the sweet communion you have with his people; the public ordinances of his house; and the prospects opened to you in the gospel of "a house not made with hands, eternal in the heavens."[24] Who can review the long catalogue of blessings secured to him as the disciple of Jesus without feeling the sacred spark already kindling in his bosom, which inflamed the host of heaven with gratitude, and teaches them with a loud voice to cry, "Worthy is the lamb that was slain, to receive power, and riches, and wisdom, and strength, and honour, and glory, and blessing. Amen."[25]

National mercies

Though the blessings we enjoy as Christians claim our highest praise, yet much gratitude is due from us as Britons; and as we are invited by the supreme magistrate to national thanksgiving, on this day, I should ill answer the end of our meeting did I not take notice of national mercies.

It is to be greatly lamented that we are more disposed to discontent on account of what we have not, than to gratitude for what we enjoy. Else should we ever cease thankfully to reflect, that we are placed in a climate so highly conducive to comfort and health—that we have been so long exempt from those fatal epidemics which in other countries, so frequently almost depopulate a district, and by which some of our acquaintance have this very year been cut off in America—that the means of decent sustenance may be attained here with as little labor, and as much certainty as in any civilized nation—that provisions are plentifully furnished from our own island, and that the divine goodness has so richly supplied us these last years, that the necessaries of life are not advanced but diminished in price—that our persons

---
[24] 2 Corinthians 5:1.
[25] Revelation 5:12.

Motives of Gratitude

and properties are protected by the laws from violence or injury—that our religious privileges, though not perfect, are so great, having Bibles in our own language, which we are allowed to read, and judge of for ourselves without the dread of a heathen tribunal, or a popish inquisition—and that we may assemble for divine worship where, and when, and how we please? Ah, had the primitive Christians, or our own ancestors, but been possessed of religious privileges equal to ours, they would have taken down their harps from the willows and cried, "Thanks be to God for these unspeakable gifts."[26]

But these are not the immediate blessings for which we are met to express our gratitude today. Recent events, in which we are all interested, are now commemorated, and I feel it my duty to point out to you the blessing for which we should now give thanks—to urge your thankfulness by suitable motives—and to direct it in its proper exercise.

I would, in the first place, state to you the precise blessing for which your thanks should now rise to heaven. Should anyone expect that I shall introduce the destruction of our foes, by the late victories gained off the coasts of Egypt and Ireland, as the object of pleasure and gratitude, he will be disappointed. The man who can take pleasure at the destruction of his fellow men, is a cannibal at heart; and for him New Zealand is a more fit habitation than civilized Europe. Let the savage secure the scalps of his enemies as monuments of his triumphs—let him collect the blood, yet smoking from their veins, and with ferocious joy quaff the sanguinary draught. But to the heart of him who calls himself a disciple of the merciful Jesus, let such pleasure be an everlasting stranger. Since in that sacred volume, which I revere as the fair gift of heaven to man, I am taught, that of one blood God has made all nations, it is impossible for me not to regard every man

---

[26] 2 Corinthians 9:15.

as my brother, and to consider that national differences ought not to excite personal animosities. Let a human soul be disembodied, and to what nation—to what colour, to what clime[27] does it then belong? Let it have tenanted what body it may, it is vast in its capacities, it is immortal in its duration; and who, with these sentiments, can reflect on the combustion of the French Admiral's ship in the late action, when a thousand immortal souls—(alas, how few prepared for the event!) were in a moment precipitated into eternity without a groan!

But though we dare not rejoice at the misery of others, we ought to be thankful for the security we enjoy ourselves. It is well known that France has long meditated and threatened a descent upon our coasts, and an invasion of our country. Proposals to this purpose have been made in her assemblies, and she has actually attempted to ensure success to her designs against us by her efforts to gain possession of Ireland, our sister kingdom. Had she succeeded in establishing her power there, where she might have victualled her fleets, and recruited her armies, England, in all probability, would have become an easy prey.

But God, the great guardian of our isle, has mercifully prevented the accomplishment of her first object. Ireland is not yet a department of France; and therefore our fears need not run high for Britain. The capture or dispersion of the ships and forces destined to that service, and the weakening the naval power of France by subsequent conquests, whereby she is rendered, as far as we can judge, incapable, for the present, of renewing her hostile attacks, are certainly occasions of real pleasure to every friend to his country, and of gratitude to every British Christian. It is then to this one object I would direct your attention the salvation of Britain from an invading power. And to excite your

---

[27] *Clime* meaning a region considered with reference to its climate.

gratitude for this, let me lay before you the following considerations:

If the French succeeded in taking Ireland
First, if the French had succeeded in taking Ireland, and had in consequence landed an hostile army on our coasts, what horrid consequences would have ensued!

What an interruption would it have occasioned to our trade and manufactures. How precarious would it have, rendered our obtaining food for our bodies. What sore anxieties and gloomy forebodings would it have excited in our bosoms. What a pause would it have put to the pleasures of social worship. Where would have been our peaceful and happy sabbaths. What tumult and disorder would it have excited among the lower orders of the people, many of whom, taking advantage of the general confusion, would have gone from house to house, plundering the peaceable inhabitants, while all, and worse than all the horrors of the former Riots, would have disgraced and distressed Birmingham. What suspicions would have existed between one inhabitant and another. What domestic misery should we have witnessed in our now tranquil dwellings—our wives and children weeping, while we, called to go out against the common foe, were taking, perhaps, a last farewell; they not knowing but we might fall in the field, and our bosoms torn with anguish, lest their honor should be violated, or the means of subsistence taken from them, so that after all our efforts to make "the present day still happier than the last," they should be abandoned to famine and death.

How dreadful would be the roar of the destructive cannon, and the din of clashing arms. What a spectacle would present itself, when, baptized in their own blood, we saw acquaintance, neighbors, kindred, friends, parents, lying in our streets; while the cries of orphans, the groans of mothers, and the shrieks of widows, completed the horror of the scene.

Good God! Who in your abundant mercy has saved us from realizing the scenes, which now only our imaginations paint, save us also from the curse of an ungrateful heart.

The moral character of our country
Secondly, let your gratitude be still heightened by reflecting on the moral character of our country, and the high demerit of its crimes.

How in this land, where God is so much known, is he also awfully blasphemed. How are his holy sabbaths profaned. How debauched in general are our youth. How luxurious the opulent.[28] And with what rapid strides does infidelity advance, while she receives a flattering welcome from all classes of Britons, from the courtier to the inhabitant of the cottage. How have the children of Christian parents declined from the piety of their ancestors. How cool is the devotion in our sanctuaries, and how many families call not upon the name of the Lord. What "sordid avarice, and low arts of commerce," stain the characters of many, eminent for rank and opulence! While in the language of a late writer:

> Our wealth and plenty have been abused to an amazing luxury, and our liberty to a boundless licentiousness. Many act as if they had no other way of showing that they are free, but by casting off all restraints, and setting themselves loose from all the ties of religion and virtue.[29]

---

[28] *Opulent* meaning rich.
[29] John Leland, *A View of the Principal Deistical Writers that Have Appeared in England in the Last Two Centuries: With Observations Upon Them, and Some Account of the Answers that Have Been Published Against Them* (London: Thomas Allman and S. Cornish, 1836), 548.

Motives of Gratitude

Who could have been surprised, if long before now, the Lord had "avenged himself on such a nation as this!" But, "slow to anger, and plenteous in mercy," while almost all Europe beside has been involved in the miseries of war, he still preserves our island a quiet habitation, and, sitting under our own vines and fig trees, none are permitted to make us afraid—"He has not dealt so with every nation; praise the Lord."[30]

Answer to prayer
Third, nor let it be forgotten, that this is a mercy granted in answer to prayer.

Often from within these walls have our fervent cries arisen to the throne of God, that he would abandon us neither to civil tumults, nor hostile foreigners; and now that he has heard our prayer, shall we refuse him praise? "O come, let us give thanks to the Lord, for he is good, for his mercy endures forever,"[31] "we cried to him, and he has helped us, and delivered us from all our fears!"[32]

Manner of expression
Lastly, while I indulge the hope that your hearts reverberate the invitation to praise, I would offer you some directions as to the manner in which you should express it:

1. Let us express our sense of obligation for national mercies, by breaking off from national sins. Let each one of us consider, that his individual crimes go towards augmenting the mass of national iniquity. Let none of us go on any longer to provoke the Lord to jealousy; and if the fear of national judgments has not power to restrain our corruptions, let a sense of national mercies engage us to repentance and reformation.

---

[30] Psalm 147:20.
[31] Psalm 136:1.
[32] Psalm 34:4.

2. Let us discover our gratitude by endeavoring to excite that of others. While the multitude, who on the one hand charge all the miseries of a nation on its governors instead of its crimes, attribute on the other all our security merely to the valor of our commanders, and their forces at sea or on land, let us strive to raise their views to a much higher cause of safety—let us teach our neighbors, our children, our servants, that "Salvation is only of the Lord."[33]

3. Let us show our gratitude to God by our benevolence to our distressed fellow creatures.

We read that when God delivered the Jews from Babylon, and days of thanksgiving were appointed; the injunction was, "Go your way, eat the fat, and drink the sweet, and send portions to them for whom nothing is prepared."[34] And when should our hearts be opened to the miseries of others, but at the moment when we are expressing our sense of the divine liberality to us; indeed he is a hypocrite, and not a sincere worshipper, who pretends to gratitude without benevolence.

But whom should we select as objects of our benevolence today? Can we think on any objects more suitable than those whose miseries are occasioned by that very event, which furnishes us with matter of joy and praise—I mean the widows and orphans of the brave men who have lately fallen in the defence of their country?

I am extremely happy to reflect that a measure has been adopted, which, in all likelihood will unite most, if not all the congregations in Birmingham, in this becoming charity. Too long separated by mutual jealousies, let us gladly embrace a proposal which breathes a spirit of conciliation, and prove by our liberality

---

[33] Acts 4:12.
[34] Nehemiah 8:10.

this day, that we are steady friends to the interests of our country, and to the interests of benevolence.

12
Letter to the Lascars[1]

1798

Lascars!

You are far from home, and in a country of strangers. Most of the Europeans you have been accustomed to observe, have perhaps discovered a desire for nothing but gain, or honour, or personal indulgence. But you know not all. In this strange land there are many who think of you, weep over you, and pray to the great Allah for you.[2] Their hearts are filled with the most affectionate concern for your happiness. Some have observed, and others have inquired after your manner of life. And they are grieved to find that your bodies, and the pursuits of this world, engage all your attention. They consider that you have immortal souls within you, and they send you this paper to beseech you to consider it with seriousness. Consider that this life is the passage to another, and that while you are unconcerned about eternity, you cannot be prepared for it.

You profess to believe that there is a God, who made you and all things. God has not made all things alike. Some creatures have no capacity for attaining the knowledge of God, as the beasts, birds, and fishes. And as they cannot know God nor his

---

[1] "Letter to the Lascars" in John Rippon, ed., The Baptist Annual Register (London, 1798-1801), 3:433-438. A Lascar was an Indian or Southeast Asian sailor. The word is a loanword from a Persian and Urdu word laškarī, meaning "soldier." Pearce wrote this excellent example of an eighteenth-century Evangelical tract in the late autumn of 1798. See Ernest A. Payne, The First Generation: Early Leaders of the Baptist Missionary Society in England and America (London: Carey Press, [1936]), 50. This chapter has been provided by Michael A.G. Haykin.

[2] Pearce here uses the term "Allah" as a term for God. Many Evangelicals today would strongly disagree with such usage.

will, so there is no good nor evil in their doings. But you, who are made capable of this great attainment, you, who must live forever, are accountable for all your actions. God hears everything you say, and sees everything you do. God knows all your thoughts, and desires, and purposes; and he will call you to an account for all at the great day when he shall judge the world in righteousness.

Were you ever concerned to know what you must do to please God? Did you ever consider that, as he gives you your life and all its comforts, you ought therefore to praise him? Do you consider that, as you are constantly dependent upon him for all things, you ought to pray to him? Consider that as he is altogether good and holy, you ought supremely to love him and delight in him. Surely, if you have never thought upon these things before, it is now high time to begin, lest you should die in your sins, and God at last should say, concerning each of you, "Here is a vile ungrateful Lascar, whom I made, and fed, and clothed, and preserved all the days of his life; but he never thought upon me, never praised me, never loved me. Cast him into hell forever!"

You believe that Moses was a prophet. By him God gave his law to man in writing. That law requires all men to love God with all their heart, and to love their neighbour as they love themselves.[3] No law could be more just than this, for God is infinitely good himself and is the author of all the good in the universe. And as to men, we are all descended from one father, and therefore we all ought to love one another as brethren. Nor could any law be given, the observance of which, would so effectually benefit ourselves; for if we love God supremely, and one another disinterestedly, we shall all be peaceful and happy, since all the misery that exists in the world is owing to nothing else but a want

---

[3] Deuteronomy 6:5.

Letter to the Lascars

of love to God and one another. And, indeed, God himself denounces the most awful vengeance on every soul that does man evil, and breaks his most good and holy law; for by the same prophet, Moses, he has declared, "Cursed is everyone who continues not in all things written in the book of the law to do them."[4]

Alas, alas! All men have broken this good law. We have broken it, you have broken it, and therefore we are all sinners under the curse of God. And, oh! what a dreadful thing it is for a rational, immortal being to be cursed by the blessed God, and cursed forever.

What then will you do to be saved? How will you escape the damnation of hell? Can you pay the debt you have contracted? Can you blot out the remembrance of your sins from the mind of God? Can you evade his search, flee from his vengeance, induce a change in his purposes, or defy his power? As well might you attempt to drain the ocean or displace the stars.

What then will you do? O, dear Lascars! we send you glad tidings of great joy. The God whom we have offended, has taken pity on us, and in his love and mercy, has raised up an all-sufficient Saviour. He is a Saviour fit for us, and fit for you; able to save us both to the uttermost,[5] to restore us to the enjoyment of God, from whom we have wandered, to fill us with a sense of his love in life, to comfort us when we are sinking in death, and to raise us to the enjoyment of immortal blessedness.

In communicating these glad tidings to you, we do not deceive you with the words of man's invention. We have the authority of the great God himself for what we say, and the experience of our own hearts assures us of its truth. Once indeed we were all like you, ignorant of our guilty and dangerous state. We

---

[4] Galatians 3:10; Deuteronomy 27:26.
[5] Hebrews 7:25.

thought only about being happy in this world, but the more we strove to be so, the more wretched we became. This came to the point when, at last, it pleased God to teach us the danger of dying as we were, and the folly of delaying, for a single moment, to search if salvation might be obtained. Our hearts were filled with fear, and we put the same question to ourselves which we have now put to you. What must we do to be saved? Then we fell down before God, and confessed that we were rebellious sinners, who had deserved his everlasting anger; and that, if he punished us forever, he would do us no wrong. We earnestly entreated him for his mercy, and besought him to show to us some way of salvation. Behold he was graciously entreated of us. He sent his word, and healed us.[6] He made known to us the way of peace; and, dispelling fear from our hearts, filled them with consolation and joy.

Now, no sooner did we taste these inestimable blessings, than, such was their nature, they begot in us the most earnest longings that every poor sinner in the world might be made as happy as ourselves.

We saw the world lying in wickedness, the far greater part of mankind living like brutes, thoughtless of themselves and God. Among these, dear Lascars, we beheld you. God, who had mercy on us, moved us to pity your unhappy state, and in sincere affection to tell you the way to be happy here, and forever.

Hear, then, Lascars! the heavenly message. "God so loved the world, that he gave his only begotten Son, that whosoever believes in him might not perish, but have everlasting life."[7] The great Gift of God to us, and for us, is Jesus Christ. You perhaps have been taught that this Jesus was only a prophet, like Moses, and could do no more for you, but you have been misled.

---

[6] Psalm 107:20.
[7] John 3:16.

The Jewish prophets who came before him most plainly foretold that he was to be a divine Saviour. His disciples, who were taught from his own lips, went about the world, declaring that they had found him of whom Moses in the law and the prophets had written, even Jesus of Nazareth, who they affirmed, as to his natural descent, came from the stock of Abraham, but who was also "God over all, blessed forever."[8] And all who heartily received their report, found, as we also have, deliverance, and peace, and joy, by believing on his name.

You allow that Jesus was God's prophet. Now he said that he and the Father were one,[9] so that they who honoured the Son did honour the Father also.[10] But the prophets of God do not lie, and therefore we adore him as the Son of God.

This blessed Saviour, for the great love that he bore to us poor sinners, from before the foundation of the world, at length clothed himself in our nature, and became bone of our bone and flesh of our flesh.[11] For he was born of a virgin, in whose womb he was formed by the power of God, on which account he was free from all sin in his nature. And when he grew up to manhood, although many who were his enemies, because he preached so faithfully against their wicked practices, continually watched him to find some evil, of which they might accuse him, yet they could find none. For the first thirty years of his life, he lived mostly in obscurity, but at length he made a more public appearance. Twice did the Holy Father give notice of his dignity, by proclaiming from heaven, "This is my beloved Son, in whom I am well pleased, hear him."[12] Then he went forth in his omnipotent goodness. He raised men to life from death and the grave, and

---

[8] Romans 9:5.
[9] John 10:30.
[10] John 5:23.
[11] Genesis 2:23.
[12] Luke 3:22; 9:35.

daily employed himself in healing all manner of sickness and diseases among the people, without a single failure. This he did in the sight of all ranks of men, for three years together. And when the fame of his miracles drew the people around him, his heart being filled with compassion and tender love to them he faithfully told them of their sins, seriously warned them of their danger, exhorted them to repent, and affectionately invited them to come to him for salvation, promising them the remission of their sins, and the gift of everlasting life.[13]

But the remission of our sins cost him most grievous sufferings, for nothing besides his precious blood was sufficient for our redemption. Yet so much was his heart set upon our salvation, that he was content to undergo the severest torments, and to die the most shameful and cruel death, rather than we should be lost forever.

This, Lascars, this is the blessed news! These are the glad tidings of great joy which must be preached to all people, and which the God of heaven, by our means, now sends to you. Jesus was crucified for us. He died that we may live. He suffered that we may be happy.

Behold, here, the mystery of his incarnation and learn why God was manifested in the flesh.[14] Had he not put on our nature, how could he have suffered in our place? And if he had not been divine, of what more value would his blood have been then the blood of one of us, or one of you?

But now we cannot doubt of the efficacy of his sufferings, who was at once the Son of God and the Son of Man. And who can but admire and adore the grace of our Lord Jesus Christ, that he should endure such agonies for us? Jesus shed his blood for the Jews, and there were thousands of the posterity of Abraham,

---

[13] Romans 6:23.
[14] 1 Timothy 3:16.

Letter to the Lascars

who believed in his name, and loved him till they died. Jesus died for Gentiles too. He died for us, and since we knew his love, our hearts have been drawn to love him in return. Jesus died for Lascars! Jesus suffered unnumbered tortures for Lascars!

O Lascars, have you no love to Jesus? Long indeed you have remained ignorant of our dear Saviour, but now God has made sailors of you, and sent you to England, that you might no longer be unacquainted with Jesus. O, how great the privilege that you hear his blessed name and are taught the truths of his great salvation before you die. Lascars, receive into your hearts this Word of life. Give thanks to God that you are not suffered to perish for want of a Saviour. Put your trust in the Almighty Jesus and yield yourselves to him as living sacrifices. Then shall you have the witness in yourselves that he is the Son of God, for you will find such peace, such joy, such delight in God, such desires after purity, such love to our Saviour and to all who love him too, of every country and of every colour, as will assure your hearts more strongly than all the force of arguments that the religion of Jesus came from heaven, and that it leads thither every soul who sincerely embraces it.

Consider, dear Lascars, this Jesus, though he died, yet he arose again to life on the third day, after which he ascended up into heaven, to dwell with his Father, and to govern the world, until he shall come the second time to judge all men, and fix their states forever. Then it will be found that those who have believed on him, and owned him before men, shall be eternally saved. But those who persist in disbelieving on his name, shall be everlastingly condemned.

Lascars, believe in the Lord Jesus Christ, and you shall be saved!

Scripture Index

Old Testament

Genesis		5:14	77
2:23	199	Ezra	
Exodus		10:10	92
20:16	3	Nehemiah	
20:17	149	8:10	192
34:6	157, 180	Esther	
Leviticus		10:3	177
13:46	175	Psalms	
14:2	176	2:2	132
Numbers		2:4-6	132
24:7	80	2:8	67
Deuteronomy		13:13	27
4:32–33	154	16:11	109
6:5	155, 196	23:4	166
27:26	197	29:3	80
31:16	27	32:5	157
Judges		34:4	157, 191
5:23	66	53	30
5:31	60	68:18	130
1 Samuel		73:25–26	179
3:1	153	73:26	166
13:14	1, 141	76:10	67
18:12	2	94:2	124
2 Samuel		103:1–2	180
1:19	38	107:20	198
6:6	20	112:4	166
1 Kings		112:6	146
4:33	178	119	153
2 Kings		119:50	166
2:12	25	119:61	1, 22

119:117	57	3:15	130, 141
136:1	191	3:22	61
139:21	31	17:10	71
145:8	180	31:33	58
147:20	191	51:13	80
148	185	Lamentations	
Ecclesiastes		2:13	39
1:18	160	3:26	67
3:1	162	5:14	38
8:2	121	Ezekiel	
9:10	65	8:14	154
Song of Songs		18:4	66
2:2	147	19	80
8:7	80	Daniel	
8:7	60	3:21	3
Isaiah		6:16	3
1:12–13	86	9:8	61
8:20	76	12:4	64
11:13	21	Hosea	
12:6	114	14:2	61
30:9–10.	144	14:4	61
38:17	157	Habakkuk	
49:14	114	2:2	161
49:16	114	3:17	166
Jeremiah		3:18	166
1:5	167	Zechariah	
3:14	61	8:23	59

Scripture Index

New Testament

Matthew		16:16	86
3:6	79	Luke	
3:11	79	1:37	138
3:15	69	2:14	180
3:16	79	3:20	79
4:23	176	3:22	199
5:21	63	9:35	199
7:2	31	10:6	63
7:20	147	10:27	155
7:21	62	12:35	67
8:32	79	14:23	150
11:29	70	16:24	77
12:20	65	17:12	175
13:3	161	17:13	176
15:14	144	17:14	176
18:15	63	17:15–16	175
19:14	90, 165	17:17–18	177
19:22	31	22:19	14, 22
24:6-7	67	24:49	131
24:12	67	John	
24:42	67	1:14	180
24:45	143	2:5	97
25:34–40	172	3:3	147
25:40	135	3:16	184, 198
27:25	91	3:23	80
28:8	158	3:36	159
28:19	77	4:2	90
28:19–20	85	4:24	143
28:20	131	5:23	199
Mark		5:39	155
1:5	79	5:40	118
10:14–16	90	6:27	62
13:8	67	6:44	118
13:35	67	6:53	96
16:15–16	85	6:69	74

8:26	77	20:24	31
10:30	199	28:17	73
11:2	25	28:22	73
11:3	26	Romans	
11:15	26	1:2	181
11:21	44	1:22	181
11:25	44	2:7	58
13:20	135	3:22	156
14:6	158	3:23	117
17:3	73	3:24	115
18:20	70	3:26	159
18:36	111	4:5	114
21:17	27	4:25	159
Acts		5:3	113
2:39	91	5:12	107
2:41	87	5:12–21	147
2:47	133	5:13	122
4:12	192	6:1–2	122, 145
5:31	159	6:4	80, 81, 83
6:4	63	6:5	46
8:12–13	87	6:14	22
8:36	79	6:23	200
8:36–38	87	8:28	166
9:1	132	8:29	58
9:18	87	8:30	115
10:38	58	9:5	199
10:44–48	87	9:15–16	115
11:19	133	11:7	65
11:23	30	12:1	61
16:14–15	87	14:19	147
16:15	88	14:23	62
16:30	182	16:17–18	147
16:32–34	89	16:23	89
16:40	88	1 Corinthians	
17:31	75	1:14	89
18:8	89	1:16	89
19:1–5	89	2:2	34
19:20	132	4:15	140

Scripture Index

6:20	62	4:12	136
7:14	91	4:13	147
9:9	140	4:15	148
9:11	139	4:24	58
9:13–14	139	5:1–2	58
9:25–26	148	5:29	135
11:1	58	6:1	163
11:29	15	Philippians	
13:8	160	1:9	151
15:58	59	1:11	151
16:13	70	1:23	43
16:15	89	1:27	149
2 Corinthians		2:1	67
1:4	113	2:1–2	151
2:14	113	2:16	148
2:16	137	3:8	161
3:5	137	3:12	135
4:2	40, 144	3:13	59
5:1	186	3:13–14	148
5:11	64	3:14	59, 158
5:17	92	Colossians	
9:15	187	1:10	146
Galatians		1:14	138
1:23	133	2:12	80
3:10	197	2:14–15	130
3:27	93	3:23	65
4:14	145	1 Thessalonians	
4:16	144	1:9	142
6:7.	121	2:19	151
Ephesians		4:14	27
1:4	121	4:16	45
1:11	117, 125	4:18	46
2:4–7	180	5:22	57
2:12	138	5:25	137
2:19	138	2 Thessalonians	
4:4–5	93	2:13	58
4:7	131	3:6	57
4:11	129, 130, 131		

1 Timothy		2:23	22, 70
1:13	157	3:8	159
1:15	15, 158	3:9	70
3:16	200	3:18	184
4:15	148	4:7	67
4:15.	138	2 Peter	
6:3	58	1:5	59
2 Timothy		1:5–7	145
3:5	162	1:10	126
3:15	153, 161, 167	1 John	
3:17	164	3:2	148
4:2	145	3:3	59
4:8	148	3:13	1
Titus		3:14	30
2:13	160	5:4	113
2:13–14	72	Jude	
2:14	58, 125	1:23	64
3:8	145	1:3	126
Hebrews		Revelation	
4:16	158	1:9.	3
7:25	197	2:4–5	60
10:20	159	5:12	186
12:14	75, 108	14:2	80
13:8	46, 133	14:13	41
James		19:13	77
1:17	134	19:15	67
5:20	146	21:3	185
1 Peter		21:27	23
1:5	109	22:7	68
2:2	148	22:12	68
2:3	64	22:20	68
2:21	58		

Further reading

The classic biography of Samuel Pearce is that by his close friend, Andrew Fuller, *Memoirs of the Late Rev. Samuel Pearce, A.M.*, 1st ed. (Clipstone: J. W. Morris, 1800). It was a best seller on both sides of the Atlantic for much of the nineteenth century, going through a number of editions and printings. For a recent reprint of this memoir, see Andrew Fuller, *The Life of Samuel Pearce* (Peterborough, ON: H&E Publishing, 2020). For a critical edition of this memoir, see Michael A.G. Haykin, ed., *Memoirs of the Rev. Samuel Pearce*, The Complete Works of Andrew Fuller, volume 4 (Berlin; Boston, MA: Walter de Gruyter, 2017).

In the early twentieth century, Pearce's great-grandson, S. Pearce Carey (1862–1953), wrote a very readable biography of his forebear, which went through three editions by 1923: *Samuel Pearce, M. A., The Baptist Brainerd*, 3rd ed. (London: The Carey Press, [1923]). More recently, Michael A.G. Haykin and Jerry Slate have co-authored a modern biography of Pearce: *Loving God and Neighbor with Samuel Pearce* (Bellingham, WA: Lexham Press, 2019).

Finally, as a companion volume to this collection of Pearce's published works is a volume of extracts from Pearce's writings, published and unpublished, and those of his wife Sarah, which reveal the shape of their spirituality: *Joy unspeakable and full of glory: The piety of Samuel and Sarah Pearce* (Kitchener, ON: Joshua Press, 2012).

Date Completed	Name

H&E Publishing
www.HesedAndEmet.com

www.ingramcontent.com/pod-product-compliance
Lightning Source LLC
Chambersburg PA
CBHW030258100526
44590CB00012B/439